Praise for *Where Hope Rises*

Lonely. Frightened. Hopeless. Devastated. Such feelings are common to those who suffer the death of a loved one or the death of a dream. How can we best help counseling clients, friends, and people we love who are walking the lonely path of grief?

Thanks to Chaplain Burghardt, we have this new comforting resource to recommend.

Each devotion stands alone as a bite-sized portion of reassurance. Hurting people need a voice like hers; one that portrays a calm, non-anxious acceptance and peaceful encouragement that God is walking this hard path beside them.

—**Charlene J. Giles, M.A., L.M.F.T.**, Former Director of Care and Marriage Ministries at Asbury United Methodist Church, Tulsa, Oklahoma

Writing a book about grief and suffering that can be helpful to a broad group of sufferers is not easy. Ms. Burghardt, however, has done just that. She writes from the perspective of someone who not only has personally experienced loss in many ways but also as a chaplain who has been given the privilege of listening to the hearts of others. As a result, this book deals with a wide range of stories, and yet, those going through grief can learn from each one. Ms. Burghardt has captured so well that there is a universality about the grief we share. I highly recommend this book as a practical guide to understanding and dealing with grief.

—**David DeKlavon, Ph.D.**, Associate Professor of New Testament Interpretation, Boyce College (retired)

For anyone who is hurting, anyone who feels lonely, anyone who is grieving, this devotional brings not only a warmth of love and kindness, but, more importantly, it brings the promise of healing of the soul from the Holy Spirit. Through her well-crafted words and stories, Rev. Burghardt shares the depth of comfort from her own personal life stories as well as from the Scriptures. Where your heart is hurting, this will help take you through the pain to the joy that awaits you.

—**Rev. Damon E. Relder**, Senior Associate Pastor,
Coker Methodist Church, San Antonio, Texas

———

Jesus said that we will have suffering in this world (John 16:33), but He promises to be with us. With the passion of an evangelist and the heart of a chaplain, Charleen Burghardt leads us through the scriptures to see the presence of God in our suffering and grief. Her openness and transparency in sharing her own journey are both beautiful and inspiring, and this book will be an invaluable resource for anyone who finds themselves in the company of heartache and loss.

—**Rev. Dr. Adam Knight**, Senior Pastor, Coker Methodist Church,
San Antonio, Texas

———

Charleen Burghardt has written a very tender and compassionate book that relates to grieving and loss in a most personal way. She knows the heaviness of loss and the heartaches that accompany loss and has found strength and comfort in her faith in God and in the truths of His Word, the Bible. This book is a gift to those who are walking in the valley of the shadow of death. Readers will benefit and be blessed by this book as they try to find hope and comfort in their losses.

—**Beverly Moore**, Certified Biblical Counselor with the Association of Certified Biblical Counselors; BA, Theology; Master's in Biblical Counseling; Coauthor of *In the Aftermath, Past the Pain of Childhood Sexual Abuse*

Charleen Burghardt's devotional is a lifeline for people, like me, who have experienced loss and grief. Throughout each devotional, Charleen is a compassionate, hope-filled guide. Her journal prompts are powerful tools for processing what is underneath the surface, getting to a place where we can allow Jesus to soothe our souls and heal our hearts. This book is more than words—it's a sacred space of restoration for the grieving.

—**Bekah Bowman**, Author of *Can't Steal My Joy* (www.bekahbowman.com)

Charleen Burghardt's devotional is a soul-soothing guide for anyone navigating grief. With the heart of a chaplain and the wisdom of lived experience, she offers tender reflections grounded in Scripture and real-life stories. This book embraces all forms of loss—death, miscarriage, divorce, chronic illness—and meets readers with honesty, grace, and hope. Each entry invites healing through prayer, reflection, and God's quiet presence. Compassionate, authentic, and beautifully written, this is a resource every grieving heart should have.

—**David F. Horkott, Ph.D.**, Associate Professor of Philosophy, Palm Beach Atlantic University

Charleen Burghardt pours out her heart in this deeply intimate journey through grief while connecting the reader to the broader hope of God. This book is inspirational and deeply practical. Through it, readers will have a chance to honestly process the complex and deep pain of loss while discovering the healing that comes when Jesus is your companion in the valley of the shadow of death.

—**Rev. Ryan Barnett**, Senior Advisor for the Advancement of the Wesley House of Studies at Truett Seminary, Coauthor of *Profoundly Christian, Distinctly Methodist*

Chaplain Burghardt has provided us with an insightful and helpful book in navigating the grief that accompanies loss. She found a relatable balance in connecting the truth of the Scriptures with her own personal experiences of grief and walking with others through it as a chaplain and caregiver. The wisdom she offers in this book will help many find hope and comfort.

—**Rev. Edmund Knot**, Director of Pastoral Care at CarolinaEast Healthcare System in New Bern, North Carolina

Charleen, thanks for a devotional that is filled with the work and struggle of grief. This devotion will help those grieving be able to find their story and not only find their story but find a way to healing. This devotion is insightful and God sent. Finally, it often said that people can follow when they know that the one that is leading understands their journey they are on. Your readers will quickly know that you understand their pain as you have had your own pain and use it to help others. Thank you for a devotion that is real and heart felt.

—**Rev. Leona D. Tatum**, Chaplain, Executive Director, Christus VNA Hospice

As a retired Pastor, I see *Where Hope Rises* penned by the Holy Spirit as a "gift" through Chaplain Charleen. God's Gift of healing is available in these pages of witness, scripture and insight. The Topical Index and the Recommended Reading List are invaluable tools for pastors as we meet and minister with those who are grieving. Charleen shares her deeply personal life experiences and the healing mercies of the power of God. I highly encourage pastors, chaplains and layfolk to incorporate *Where Hope Rises* as a valuable tool in the life of your ministry.

—**Reverend Sue White**, Retired Elder, Global Methodist Church

This well-crafted devotional offers thoughtful guidance for those navigating grief and loss. Drawing from personal experience and chaplaincy ministry, the author provides biblical reflection, practical encouragement, and space for personal response. Recognizing that grief arises from many. kinds of loss - death, disability, divorce, dreams deferred, and more—this is a valuable resource for individuals and ministries seeking to support those in these seasons of heartache.

—**Terri Stovall, Ph.D.**, Dean of Women: Professors of Educational Ministries, Southwestern Baptist Theological Seminary

I am so grateful to my sister in Christ for writing this very important book. With 60 reflections written from Charleen's personal experiences as a Pastor and Chaplain, she explores the key components of pastoral care around the various forms of grief. This is an excellent resource for individuals and clergy who are seeking healing or to be in ministry to someone who needs healing.

—**Bishop Leah Gregory**, Bishop Global Methodist Church, and Superintendent of MidTexas Conference

WHERE
hope
RISES

60 Devotions for Walking
Through Grief with God

CHARLEEN BURGHARDT

ILLUMIFY
MEDIA.COM

Published by
Illumify Media Global
www.IllumifyMedia.com
"Let's bring your book to life!"

Library of Congress Control Number: 2025909370

Paperback ISBN: 978-1-964251-67-7

Typeset by Art Innovations (http://artinnovations.in/)
Cover design by Debbie Lewis
Page Ornament by Jaclyn Blackberby

Printed in the United States of America

Contents

How to Use This Book

EACH DEVOTION STARTS with a key Scripture, followed by a story or illustration about loss that ties to the Scripture. After the devotion prompts are provided to help you process and reflect.

- A prayer
- A prompt to reflect
- A call to respond to the devotion
- Suggested additional Scripture reading
- A journal prompt, which will be a powerful tool to process your feelings or an avenue to invite God into your sadness. A place to journal is provided or you may want to use your own journal.

You can read this devotional from beginning to end or alternatively, pick a different topic each day. Allow yourself time to ponder, linger, and digest the words in the Scripture and devotion. As you continue to process your grief, you may find it helpful to return and read the devotions again later—they might speak to you in new and deeper ways over time. The back of the book includes a topical index, a recommended reading list, and a guide on how to connect with Jesus. My prayer is that God will use this devotional to bring comfort through your loss and the strength as needed. May you sense God holding you as you read these pages.

Introduction

EARLY IN MY chaplain ministry, I met a woman in her late sixties who was seriously ill. Her face contorted in pain, her gray hair tangled, and her shoulders slumped as she sat propped up in bed. After introducing myself, I asked, "What's happening?"

In a broken, raspy voice, she replied, "The doctors tell me I am in serious condition. I can't walk and have trouble breathing. My diabetes and weak heart are complicating my recovery."

As I listened and prayed silently, I sensed a gentle kindness in her. Her concern stretched beyond herself to her unwell daughter and a grandchild in a challenging situation. "I have little hope of getting better, and I am concerned about my family," she said resignedly.

"I believe in God," she confessed, "but I don't understand what is happening with all of this." She spoke of her faith, although despair was evident in her voice.

"Your situation reminds me of Job in the Bible, who lost his wealth, family, and health," I said.

"Yes, I feel like Job," she said.

Gazing deeply into her hazel eyes, I said, "God was with Job, and he is with you as well. Just like with Job, God will hear your needs and take care of you. You are not alone."

She nodded, her voice barely a whisper. "I need God to hear my prayers."

While holding her hand, I prayed with her, asking the Lord to give her peace and healing. After I squeezed her hand, I said, "God bless you," and walked out of her hospital room.

A few days later, I revisited her. To my surprise, her demeanor had brightened, and she sat up straighter in bed. Though her health had only slightly improved, something had shifted in her attitude. "Chaplain, I thought about Job, and it comforted me," she said. I could see hope in her eyes and hear strength in her voice.

Throughout our lives, we all face different kinds of small and large losses. Much of our time is spent acquiring things that give our lives meaning—whether it's a spouse, a partner, friends, a career, a home, children, or financial stability. When we lose someone or something significant, we endure heartbreak, which can bring a mix of emotions—sadness, anger, disappointment, guilt, hopelessness, resentment, depression, anxiety, fear, and despair.

Like the story of the seriously ill woman above, I will walk alongside you as a chaplain during your time of loss in this devotional. Together, we will journey, guided by the Holy Spirit. This book offers comfort for anyone grappling with deep sorrow or distress following a significant loss, such as the death of a loved one. Loss brings grief—a painful experience that impacts our emotions, body, mind, and spirit, often stirring up many unexpected feelings. We are compelled to face these emotions and care for them. In addition, coping with loss challenges our sense of self and the normalcy we once knew.

Whether your grief is recent or ongoing, these devotions will help you work through your sadness and provide you with the courage and hope you need. It will give you space to grieve, provide tools to process your feelings, and guide you through steps to find healing. Grief often follows the loss of:

- Family member, partner, friend
- Neighbor, coworker
- Marriage
- A move
- Career, job
- Financial stability
- A dream or a goal
- Good health
- Your youth
- Fertility

To help you navigate the depths of your grief, I've created this devotional book filled with grief support, heartfelt faith stories, and uplifting promises from Scripture. I've woven in chaplain concepts as tools to guide you through your journey of loss. Grief is often called work because it takes great courage to face the pain of loss. We struggle with the emotions, challenges, and difficulties that come with grief. The biblical character Job did the difficult work of grieving, which led him to reevaluate his faith. Like Job, after we do the hard work of grieving, we emerge stronger, and though the sting of grief may remain, it becomes more bearable.

We frequently think God is far away, but consider this devotional as a light toward a loving God who sees, hears, and knows us thoroughly. No two people are alike; thus, I have included topics on various types of loss. This devotional can also hold your doubts and questions, allowing you to grapple with your faith. We may cry out as David did, "Why, my soul, are you downcast? Why so disturbed within me?" (Psalm 42:5).

While the words in this book can't erase your sorrow, they will validate your emotions, remind you that you are not alone, and guide you toward comfort in Christ. As you journey through these pages, you'll discover profound truths about the grieving process that will support you along the way. Remember, grief softens with time. The dark clouds of sorrow don't last forever; the pain becomes more manageable, and eventually, the memories will bring more smiles than tears. Out of cracks in our broken hearts, a bloom of hope will rise.

My Journey Through Grief

I didn't sign up for the loss, but the loss seemed to find me in my twenties. My grief journey began when I learned my two young sons showed signs of developmental delays. I worried when they were behind in the developmental markers of sitting, crawling, and walking. Within a few years, after many doctors, we discovered they had a rare chronic disease—central diabetes insipidus—that may have caused multiple disabilities.

At each of their milestones, I mourned as my peers were having healthy babies with typical development. The reality of having children with disabilities hit me hard, leaving me reeling from its impact. The disease required the services of many doctors and specialists and hospitalizations. Because their learning, speech, and motor skills were affected, I worked hard to get them into the best special education program possible. Besides cooking for special diets, I became their educator, therapist, and medical manager. Parental grief overwhelmed me. I fluctuated between anxiety, anger, denial, guilt, depression, and fear. Their illnesses shattered my dreams for them to have healthy, regular lives.

In addition to grieving, the physical demands of their care consumed me, leaving me with little time for myself and feeling lost and alone. I'd fall into bed exhausted, only able to pray, "*Help, God!*" Through a handicapped sports group, I found other parents of children with special needs who walked a similar journey, many of whom had older children, and they gave me incredible support.

I enjoyed teaching elementary school but also directed my energy toward advocacy for people with special needs. I advocated for improved educational services, served on advisory boards, worked to change laws, educated doctors on the early detection of special needs, and established a special needs summer camp. I also collaborated with an art organization to support children and adults with disabilities in the arts, which involved partnerships with school districts, art organizations, and the city. In addition, I taught classes for the National Alliance on Mental Illness.

After losing my marriage, I learned through genetic testing that I didn't carry the gene that caused my sons' disease. When I remarried, I decided to have another child since I was not a carrier of the disease. I became pregnant, but tragically, I lost the baby because of an accident in my classroom. At first, numbness and shock overwhelmed me, and then a lack of energy and motivation seemed to pervade. Nothing had prepared me for how I collapsed under the weight of sadness. I read everything available, trying to understand my emotions and how to work through them. Why did this miscarriage impact me so profoundly? After the school year finished, a depression surrounded me. I realized my miscarriage was the death of a dream for a child I had hoped for.

Another loss came when my sons developed mental health issues as adults. In order to help them connect with services, I quit teaching. I still grieve today for all they lost because of their disease, disabilities, and mental illness.

Unexpected losses continued to unfold when I lost my two best friends to cancer and my parents in their eighties. In one particularly devastating year, I experienced eight deaths within just twelve months, leaving me feeling as though I had hit a wall.

However, I asked the Lord, *How do you want to use all this pain?* From that question, I attended Southwestern Baptist Theological Seminary, earning a master of arts in Christian education. Then, I trained as a chaplain, involving a residency (six units of clinical pastoral education). I became a board-certified chaplain with the Association of Professional Chaplains. While working for over a decade as a chaplain in hospice care and the hospital, I volunteered as coordinator of my church's pastoral care and prayer ministries. In 2023 I became ordained as a Global Methodist elder.

Currently, I lead grief groups, present workshops called Grief Through the Holidays, lead holiday remembrance services, speak, teach Bible studies, and lead trainings. I write biweekly for Our Scarlett Stories, an online community dedicated to those who experience pregnancy loss. My writings have appeared in publications such as *The Upper Room, Breakthrough Intercessors Magazine,* and *Mommies Enduring Neonatal Death.* I also write for online publications such as *Christian Devotion and Arise.*

Part 1

When the Storm Hits

Day 1

Finding Hope in Grief

"Let us hold unswervingly to the hope we profess,
for he who promised is faithful."

—Hebrews 10:23

THOUGHT FOR THE DAY

We find hope in knowing God is faithful.

WILL WINTER EVER *end?* I ask myself. February feels like the longest month of the year because of its unpredictable weather, chilly temperatures, relentless wind, and persistent gray skies. The sight of bare trees without green buds evokes a sense of sadness within me. Spring seems far away.

When we have had a loss, it feels like February with no sight of spring. To add to our discouragement, well-meaning friends will tell us to overcome our grief, that life must move on. When said to us, these words are not helpful but only add to our frustration. "Time heals wounds," they say. We respond, "Oh, that time would heal my wounds quickly." We wish time would speed up and wonder if we will ever heal. Time moves at a snail's pace when we grieve.

Then the first signs of spring comes when unexpectedly bluebonnets pop up in cool temperatures. Shortly after new green vegetation appears. Grasses grow, and trees bud. Each year, I am amazed at this phenomenon.

Similarly, grief from a loss can seem like a prolonged winter with no relief in sight or no possibility of hope. Resembling the dead of winter, we experience dark days of sorrow when we grieve and find no hope. Our inability to perceive God mirrors our inability to see seeds germinate. Nevertheless, as we allow space and time for grief, something happens. God walks alongside us, gently comforting us, and working in the deep soil of our souls.

Hope arrives when we least expect it, much like spring arrives. Despite its small beginning, hope comes like the first bud of spring.

Likewise, when Jesus walked the earth and the Romans crucified him, the disciples scattered in fear, and they seemed hopeless in the darkness of Christ's death and burial. Despair, dejection, doubt, and confusion overwhelmed his followers. Questions arose, making the idea of a Messiah seem impossible.

Then, miraculously, Jesus arose from the dead. Easter morning brought renewed expectation and life. A resurrected Savior provided the possibility of forgiveness and eternal life.

Grief does not extinguish hope. God remains faithful and brings hope, as he did with the disciples that first Easter morning. In faith, we hold on to his faithfulness, even when our trust seems insignificant. With expectation, courage follows as with the beginnings of springtime, a tender growth of promise will surface from the barren earth.

Hope often begins with recognizing God's faithfulness, mercy, and promises. Expressing gratitude for God's goodness fosters hope and promotes healing.

---

*"Winter's loss leads to the spring
of recovery."*

—Jerry Sittser

Dear God of hope,

Thank you for seeing my bereavement and recognizing my heartache. I feel alone, and encouragement seems dim, yet you remain faithful and good. Cause new expectations to sprout in my heart. Amen.

Respond: Thank Jesus for coming and for the promise that God will never leave you.

Reflect: Reflect on the Lord's kindness.

Read: Psalm 36:5–10

Journal Prompt: Tell how God has been faithful to you when you asked for comfort.

Day 2

Never Alone

"Never will I leave you; never will I forsake you."

—Hebrews 13:5

THOUGHT FOR THE DAY

God is always present in our situation.

LONELINESS TAKES ON a whole new meaning after losing a loved one. Your loved one is missing day and night. We talk to them but hear no reply, and we reach out to touch them, only to be aware of their absence. We realize that we are alone, without the one we love. Nothing can replace the emptiness we feel or the longing for their companionship and conversation. For me, loneliness and grief crash in on me with no warning, knocking me off my feet and causing me to gasp for air. Have you encountered the depths of isolation crashing in on you?

One biblical example of someone who experienced loneliness is Jacob. He left his country of origin and his family when he was forty after he stole his brother Esau's inheritance. As a result, Jacob loses his bond with Esau, his twin, and gains Esau's anger. In fear for his life, Jacob traveled alone through the desert on a long expedition of 450 miles to his uncle's home. Undoubtedly, the journey seemed lengthy and desolate, with only a walking stick by his side for company. What was Jacob's emotional response when the sky turned black? Loneliness and emptiness for his father and mother? Grief for the lost relationship with his sibling and his homeland?

With only the stars and moon as light, Jacob eventually drifted off to sleep. During his slumber, God appeared in a dream of a staircase. At the top of the staircase stood the Lord, who promised to care for him. Moreover, God said to him, "I am with you" (Genesis 28:15). Jacob was given a divine promise that night, and he would hold on to that promise for the rest of his life. Furthermore, God stood by Jacob's side and with him in every trial Jacob encountered. Beyond Jacob's own life, God made him the father of twelve sons who became the nation of Israel.

Besides the assurance given to Jacob, we find another affirmation of the divine presence in the New Testament. "Never will I leave you; never will I forsake you" (Hebrews 13:5). This assurance is an extraordinary gift, not based on our merit but freely given. God's presence will always remain with us on lonely nights, during daily activities, or in a noisy crowd. Regardless of our circumstances or emotional state, God stands by our side. The Divine Creator walks with you and will never abandon you!

"No matter your situation, God is always with you. You are never entirely alone when you know Christ."

—Billy Graham

Ever-present God,

Enter our grief and loneliness. May we sense your presence in the daylight and the night's darkness. Thank you for your promise to always be with us. Be our companion in loneliness and our light in the darkness. Amen.

Respond: With expectation, wait for God to give you peace in his presence.

Reflect: Think of times when God was real to you.

Read: Psalm 139:1-12

Journal Prompt: When do you feel most lonely? Tell God about it.

Day 3

The Compassion of Christ

"When he saw the crowds, he had compassion on them, because they were harassed and helpless, like sheep without a shepherd."

—Matthew 9:36

THOUGHT FOR THE DAY

Jesus is our companion in grief.

FLORENCE NIGHTINGALE, A trailblazer in nursing, promoted personal bedside care for patients. She left a life of luxury in Britain to help wounded soldiers recover in the Crimean War in 1845. During the day, she checked on both officers and ordinary soldiers. With a lamp at night, Nightingale checked on the men's well-being in the wards. She attended to the patients' physical and emotional needs, often writing letters for them and listening to their concerns. Being present with her patients improved the soldiers' physical well-being and morale. Nightingale's bedside manner showed tangible compassion and left a legacy for nurses to follow today.

Similarly, when we experience the loss of a loved one, we have physical needs: meals delivered, someone to run errands and accompany us to an appointment. Caring for our bodies through sufficient sleep and consistent eating provides us with the energy to handle grief. However, we also have emotional needs in grief. A compassionate friend can provide emotional care with a hug or a listening ear. We have a driving desire to talk about our loved ones or cry with a friend. We want someone to be present with us.

When I lost my mother, a friend came by to deliver a meal, and then she sat with me while I showed her pictures of my mother. What a gift my friend gave me that day. She was a compassionate Florence Nightingale who sat with me in my sorrow.

Scripture provides insight into how Jesus showed compassion. During Jesus' earthly ministry, groups gathered to hear him teach and came to receive healing. He felt sympathy for the crowd because of their helplessness. Within the multitude, Jesus recognized individual needs, empathized with their suffering, and responded to those needs. He healed a man with leprosy, cast out demons from a man suffering from bondage, offered hope, dined with sinners, and fed those who were hungry.

Most importantly, in our grief, Jesus empathizes with our loss, senses our sorrow, and is filled with compassion. The Savior notices us within the crowd and responds with a deep understanding of our aching souls. Like a shepherd searching for a lost sheep, Jesus seeks us out. He comes alongside us to guide, protect, comfort, reassure, and impart peace. In addition, Jesus listens well and remains a constant, compassionate companion.

"Christ literally walked in our shoes and entered into our affliction."

—Timothy Keller

Dear Savior,

Thank you for seeing me in a crowd. You know my grief and hear my cries and prayers. In your compassion, walk with me in my grief. Amen.

Respond: Reach out to someone hurting by expressing empathy or find a Florance Nightingale.

Reflect: When have you sensed Jesus' compassion?

Read: Matthew 9

Journal Prompt: If Jesus were here, what would you tell him?

Dark Valley

"Even though I walk through the darkest valley,
I will fear no evil, for you are with me;
your rod and your staff, they comfort me."

—Psalm 23:4

MANY INDIVIDUALS FIND that grief from a loss feels like navigating a wilderness without a clear path. The loss of a beloved spouse, friend, child, or even the loss of a career can bring overwhelming sorrow mingled with disillusionment. Unexpected obstacles and twists fill the wilderness, where we neither see where we stand nor where we're going. Grief often proves more challenging than anticipated, defying our attempts to hurry through it. We may feel profoundly alone in this wilderness of grief, with no hope in sight, like being trapped in an abyss of sadness.

When we mourn the loss of a loved one or experience another kind of loss, it can seem like the mourning journey is prolonged and takes us into a deep valley with high mountains obscuring the sun. Psalm 23 uses the image of a dark valley to describe a time of trouble, which could be grief. This psalm is often called "The Lord Is

My Shepherd" because it relates a shepherd to the Lord and sheep to us. The Shepherd cares for his sheep, leading them to places of rest and nourishment and guiding them with his staff.

Also, the herdsman leads the lambs into unknown terrains without leaving them. In verse 4, the psalmist writes, "Even though I walk through the darkest valley, I will fear no evil, for you are with me." This description of a shepherd walking with sheep portrays God as a constant companion in our dark valley of sorrow.

Following the analogy of a shepherd guiding his sheep with a staff, our Shepherd leads us to safety. No matter how scary and looming the journey seems, we have the reassurance that God guides us, leading and protecting us. Our Shepherd sees us and hears us in the dark valley.

Finally, healing enters that valley. It may not be immediately apparent, but God meets us in the valley of grief with his presence to comfort our souls and spirits. We learn trust and patience while divine strength holds us up. A glimmer of hope sustains us. We have a Good Shepherd to walk with us on our grief journey, no matter how difficult.

"The Lord's mercy often rides to the door of our heart upon the black horse of affliction."

—Charles Spurgeon

Dear Good Shepherd,

Thank you for being with me in the depths of grief. You are aware of my whereabouts wherever I go. Guide me and comfort me. Let me know I am not alone. Send hope on those days of despair. Be my Shepherd and lead me to a peaceful place. Amen.

Respond: Memorize Psalm 23.

Reflect: When you lay your head on the pillow, imagine the Shepherd walking beside you.

Read: John 10:1–18

Journal Prompt: Tell God about your dark valley and what challenges you most.

Day 5

Blessed Are Those Who Mourn

"Blessed are those who mourn, for they will be comforted."

—Matthew 5:4

THOUGHT FOR THE DAY

It's okay to mourn.

HAVE YOU EVER thought, I've moved on. The death is behind me, and grief is over, and then, by surprise, something hits you about your loved one? Hot tears stream down your cheeks without warning, so much for being done with grieving.

Unexpected snuffles streamed gently down my cheeks when the aroma of cinnamon sticks filled the air and I gazed at twinkling Christmas lights. My parents will not be with me this year. I thought enough time had elapsed since their deaths. My grief has softened somewhat, but it is still there. Little did I realize that the familiar melodies of carols would trigger sad feelings.

I've come to understand that mourning doesn't possess a magical ending. Rather than thinking of grief ending, think of it as waves with fluctuations. In the same way that the ocean's tides ebb and flow, I go through dark days filled with regret and sadness and other days without sorrow. As a result, special dates, such as anniversaries, holidays, and birthdays, activate another fresh wave of sorrow, causing me to stumble backward. Often, these festive occasions present the challenges of knowing my loved ones are no longer with me. Instead of joy, I feel sadness. Sweet memories of times with them surface, and then sadness envelops me with an intense longing for them. I experience an emptiness without them and have realized that holidays aren't always like a Hallmark movie.

When we experience a feeling of sadness, we can cling to two crucial truths: we are not alone because God is with us and God understands the pain of loss. We can see these truths in the beatitude where Jesus blesses those who mourn. Besides Jesus giving a blessing of "blessed are those who mourn," a promise of comfort follows in the second half of this beatitude, "for they will be comforted." The word *comfort* conveys the idea of an embrace. One of the most consoling acts anyone can do for me when my grief brings deep heartache is to surround me with a warm hug, assuring me I am not alone. The Son of God promises to hold us.

When another unfriendly wave of sadness strikes us, we are not alone, for the Holy Spirit accompanies and comforts us. We can ask and trust that consolation, support, and encouragement will come. Hold on to this hope of blessing and comfort that Jesus gave us. Let him embrace you. "Blessed are those who mourn, for they will be comforted" (Matthew 5:4).

"Mental pain is less dramatic than physical pain, but it is more common and also more hard to bear."

—C. S. Lewis

Dear Jesus,

Be our comfort in mourning.
Be our healer in brokenness.
Be our hope in distress.
Be our guiding light in uncertainty.
Be our calm in anxiety.
Be our strength in weakness.
Be our companion in loneliness.
Thank you. Amen.

Respond: Thank God for the promise of comfort.

Reflect: Permit yourself to grieve.

Read: John 11:30–36

Journal Prompt: Describe a time when you have felt the warmth of God's embrace.

Part 2

Comfort in the Storm

Day 6

No Limit to God's Faithfulness

"Because of the LORD's great love we are not consumed,
for his compassions never fail. They are new every morning;
great is your faithfulness."

—Lamentations 3:22–23

THOUGHT FOR THE DAY

God's compassion is new every morning.

THE OLD FAITHFUL Geyser in Yellowstone National Park erupts daily and is known as one of the most predictable geysers in the United States. Visitors come from around the world to watch it expelling water over a hundred feet in the air. This dynamic wonder of nature occurs when rainwater and snow seep into the ground, where volcanic activity is far below the surface. Thermal energy creates pressure, and the geyser spouts boiling water with tremendous force.

Early explorers named the geyser Old Faithful because of its long history of erupting and its predictability. Even today, tourists can search online for the times of eruptions. This wonder of the nature of hydrothermal energy remains consistent from year to year. Like the geyser, God is faithful. The dictionary defines faithful as steadfast, true to facts, and adhering to promises.

The prophet Jeremiah spoke to the Jews when they grieved the destruction of Jerusalem. They experienced enormous loss, suffering, and pain, leading to great mourning. Amid their sorrow, Jeremiah spoke of God's faithfulness. He reminded them that God remained with them and was loyal to them. From his words, hope emerged. They gained new strength in their faith and assurance that God heard them and was present.

Likewise, we can call on the one who hears in our time of mourning. We can count on God to come through and to get us through. When we look at our circumstances, and especially when we have a loss, it causes us to feel alone and hopeless. It is very human to grieve a loss and to think no one else knows what we are going through. Grief is unpredictable, but God, unlike grief, is steadfast. Those are the times we can fix our gaze on the faithful one, pray, and be assured he hears.

In addition, God's compassion and mercy never waver. Like clockwork, new mercies greet us daily as we leave our beds. No matter how we feel, we can call on a dependable God to meet us in our sorrow. Grief and loneliness may engulf us, but new mercies await us every morning. God faithfully sympathizes with our loss, has compassion for us, and hears our prayers.

"It's possible to go on, no matter how impossible it seems, and that in time, the grief lessens. It may not go away completely, but after a while it's not so overwhelming."

—Nicholas Spark

Faithful God,

I feel alone in my loss. Hear my prayer today for comfort in my sorrow. I need your mercies to face the day and get me through what is ahead. I need your grace to hold me up. May I sense your compassionate presence with me. Amen.

Respond: Thank God for new mercies each day.

Reflect: Listen to or read the words of the old hymn "Great Is Thy Faithfulness."

Read: Psalm 36:5–12

Journal Prompt: Recall and list times when you have seen the faithfulness of God this week.

Day 7

Tear Collector

"You keep track of all my sorrows. You have collected all my tears in your bottle. You have recorded each one in your book."

—Psalm 56:8 NLT

> **THOUGHT FOR THE DAY**
>
> Our tears matter to God.

HOW OFTEN HAVE we heard phrases like "Don't cry" or "Get over it!" after going through a loss? These words can make us feel as though we need to hide or suppress our grief. However, whether others are comfortable with our tears or not, crying is a natural way to express emotions and release tension. Research shows that crying releases oxytocin and endorphins, which can help alleviate emotional pain. In this way, tears play a crucial role in processing and healing after a loss, serving as a vital outlet for our emotions.

Moreover, Scripture provides accounts of weeping as a means of expressing grief. One account tells of a faithful man named Job who lost his possessions, his means of income, and his children. He lost all his livestock through several catastrophes, his offspring perished in a horrific disaster, and painful boils covered his body. Three friends sat with Job in mourning, but they judged him instead of offering comfort, encouragement, and strength. They failed to see Job's need to grieve. Yet Job describes his intense grief by saying, "My face is red with weeping, dark shadows ring my eyes" (Job 16:16 NLT). Job's weeping gave him a way to mourn.

Can you relate to Job with bloodshot and puffy eyes? We find other examples in the book of Psalms, which describes tears as a way to mourn. For instance, the bottle metaphor illustrates how deeply our tears matter to God. He even collects them in a bottle. Just as a rain gauge collects water, God gathers and stores our tears in his divine jar. Each drop of moisture that runs down our face matters to the living God. No sob goes unnoticed or forgotten.

When we are overwhelmed by grief, it's okay to let our tears stream unhindered and without shame. Tears are a healthy release and a means of grieving, providing a beneficial method of letting go of our raw emotions. Indeed, when we possess no words but tears, God hears.

Someday, all tears will be gone when the new heaven and earth come. "There will be no more death or mourning or crying or pain, for the old order of things has passed away" (Revelation 21:4).

"It is okay to let the tears come, to weep over all this pain, all this love, all this beauty, all this brokenness. . . . Sometimes you can't experience full recovery until you let your pain be fully uncovered."

—Ann Voskamp

Dear Tear Collector,

My pain has no words today, only tears. Thank you for valuing my gentle tears, bitter sobs, and uncontrollable weeping. Comfort me with the sweetness of your presence. Amen.

Respond: Be thankful for the tears of sorrow you cry, for they are a release.

Reflect: Reflect on when you felt better after you shed tears. Allow time and find a place for your prayers to run down your cheeks.

Read: Psalm 34:15-22

Journal Prompt: Describe when you were most tearful in the last few weeks.

Day 8

The Lord Is My Shepherd

"The LORD is my shepherd, I lack nothing.
He makes me lie down in green pastures,
he leads me beside quiet waters, he refreshes my soul."

—Psalm 23:1–3

THOUGHT FOR THE DAY

Jesus is our Good Shepherd.

AS A CHILD, I lived in an old farmhouse that creaked with noises, and the wind whistled through the old boards. At night, darkness filled my upstairs bedroom, illuminated only by the light of the moon and stars. It could be eerie for a child. My imagination would run wild, and my stomach would tighten, keeping me from drifting off. I found a treasure in Psalm 23 that helped me fall asleep. In fact, I memorized the psalm as the first verses I ever committed to memory. The verse "The Lord is my shepherd" settled my mind and heart.

I meditated on the verses from Psalm 23, envisioning a shepherd leading me to a restful place, picturing a lush meadow beside a tranquil river. The rich imagery of God as a shepherd gave me a sense of protection. Then I considered myself a lamb cherished by the Good Shepherd who cared for my needs. Even today, I often remind myself that I am valued and held by Jesus when a dark cloud of sadness hangs over me.

In life, unexpected and tragic events happen that we don't understand or can't control. Preventing a disease, an accident, or a natural disaster is usually impossible. When a loved one dies of cancer, no effort can bring them back. Nor can words ease the pain of loss. A feeling of helplessness overwhelms us while the burden of our grief weighs heavily.

Since certain challenging circumstances in life are beyond our control, we can look to our Shepherd, who soothes us with gentle care and understanding. Jesus referred to himself as the Good Shepherd in John 10. He watches over his sheep—us—and never forsakes us. Imagine Jesus standing close by our side when weeping continues through the night and our bodies tremble. We can envision Jesus receiving us into his warm, solid embrace. As we let those thoughts wash over us, peace permeates us, much like the tranquility we experience while strolling through quiet woods.

"The Good Shepherd provides all we need.
No matter the trial or the ache of loss,
Jesus is always present, holding us."

—Charleen Burghardt

Dear God, my Good Shepherd,

Lead me to restful places, such as green pastures and quiet streams. Please give me the calm I need when grief and fears surge in. Hold me when I am weak and unable to go forward. May I experience your comforting presence. Amen.

Respond: In times of fear, gaze upon the Good Shepherd.

Reflect: Imagine Jesus as the Good Shepherd, receiving your loved one into his arms.

Read: John 10:1–16

Journal Prompt: Write a letter to the Shepherd about what you fear most.

Day 9

The Throne of Grace

*"Let us then approach God's throne of grace with confidence,
so that we may receive mercy and find grace
to help us in our time of need."*

—Hebrews 4:16

Thought for the Day

We can approach God with confidence.

NOT ALL GRIEF is from death, and so I discovered when I had my two older sons, both born with a rare disease, who later developed multiple disabilities. Because of this, I didn't know what to call the sadness, the regret, and the roller coaster of emotions until I attended a conference for parents of children with special needs. The speaker identified many of the feelings I experienced as grief and permitted me to have those feelings.

Later, I learned the term *non-death loss,* referring to loss that is not from a physical death. In other words, I mourned for what my sons lost from having a chronic illness. When they were young, I made the best of the situation and turned medical appointments and therapies into outings. Their lives revolved around their health and special education.

In those early years, I couldn't find the vocabulary to express my inner grief, and at times, the sadness didn't have words. I uttered simple prayers, asking for grace and mercy. God heard those pleas, gave me what I needed daily, and comforted me in my grief.

All of us go through sorrow in life, whether it is the death of someone we love or relinquishing something we value, such as a career, health, or a dream. We can feel misunderstood and fragile in those losses, but Scripture assures us that Jesus understands. When Jesus walked on Earth, he endured the same trials that we endure and thus understood our emotional pain. "For we do not have a high priest who is unable to empathize with our weaknesses" (Hebrews 4:15).

Because Jesus made a way for us to reach God and fully understands our weaknesses and challenges, we can draw near to the throne of grace with confidence. The invitation remains open and available at all times. There, we find not only grace and mercy but also deep understanding and compassion. Grace is God's limitless love and unearned favor, providing all we require. Mercy offers forgiveness and pardon we could never earn, extended with heartfelt empathy.

Above all, we can release all our spoken and unspoken emotions to the one who understands and asks for divine strength, comfort, hope, peace, and everything we require each day.

"Christ went more willingly to the cross than we do to the throne of grace."

—Thomas Watson

Dear gracious and merciful God,

I come to the throne of grace and in my weakness, may your strength carry me. Bend your ear to my whispers and wordless sobs. Be present with abundant mercy and grace. Amen.

Respond: Take your needs and brokenness to the throne of grace.

Reflect: Reflect on what it means for Jesus to understand your weakness.

Read: 1 John 5:14–15

Journal Prompt: Where do you need grace in your life? Where do you need mercy today?

Day 10

Living Water

*"Whoever believes in me, as Scripture has said,
rivers of living water will flow from within them."*

—John 7:38

WHEN VISITING ZION National Park, my family and I stayed in a small rustic cabin in the lodge area. Stark, imposing mountains framed the basin, making us seem insignificant. As far as the eye could gaze, varying rock formations, known for their red peaks and lofty cliffs, created a canyon encircling us. We had a sense of wonder in this high desert. Since we visited in the fall, crimson, yellow, and orange leaves adorned the trees. We also observed plants and animal life in the middle of this arid landscape. However, I wondered what sustained life in this rugged terrain.

One day, we hiked up a trail called Weeping Rock. After a steep climb, where we had to catch our breath several times, we noticed a rock hanging above our heads. Lush green ferns and vibrant grasses surrounded the wet crag. Upon closer examination, we witnessed crystal-clear water gently flowing from a crack in the rock. We stood in awe of this seemingly impossible water source. I'd discovered the source of the area's abundant plants and wildlife.

On my way home, I pondered the water flowing from an unexpected and unseen underground reservoir. From the reservoir, a spring bubbled up from the ground, and that spring reminded me of Jesus' conversation with a woman about giving her living water.

While traveling through Samaria, Jesus stopped at a well at midday to ask a woman for water. He then spoke of a different kind of water that takes away thirst. Jesus told her of the water he gives: "But whoever drinks the water I give them will never thirst. Indeed, the water I give them will become in them a spring of water welling up to eternal life" (John 4:14). Jesus used water as a metaphor for spiritual sustenance and salvation.

In the same way, Jesus offers spiritual refreshment in our wilderness of grief. The grief journey can feel like a vast desert, where our throats become parched and no hope seems apparent. We ask, *When will this dryness end?* Laughter doesn't come easily, and simple things no longer bring the same joy they once did. When our resources fail, Jesus invites us into a relationship with him. Christ gives hope, offering living water that revives and quenches thirst. As we draw from the well of living water, we can provide living water to others.

Invite Jesus to give you living water.

"The 'rivers of living water' Jesus was referring to is the Spirit of God working in and flowing out of the life of a believer."

—Clarence L. Haynes Jr.

Dear life-giving God,

I am in a dry place in my grief. I need living water to quench my thirst and refresh my spirit. May the Holy Spirit give me all that I need. In Jesus' name, amen.

Respond: Give to another the hope Christ gave you.

Reflect: What do you think and feel when you see a flowing stream?

Read: John 4:1–14

Journal Prompt: Write a prayer asking God to refresh you in your grief.

Day 11

Holding God's Hand

"For I am the LORD your God who takes hold of your right hand and says to you, Do not fear; I will help you."

—Isaiah 41:13

THOUGHT FOR THE DAY

We are always in God's hands.

THE BEATLES ACHIEVED worldwide fame through their unique music and romantic lyrics in the bestselling single "I Want to Hold Your Hand." As penned in this ballad, holding hands makes one feel happy, demonstrating how significant this simple connection is in expressing affection.

Besides romance, grasping hands together offers a physical connection for humans from life as a newborn to one's last dying moments. A baby's hand curls around their mother's finger as an automatic reflex. A father holds a child's hand for safety and guidance as they cross the street. Friends show their bond of loyalty when they walk hand in hand. In times of fear, with a new diagnosis, fingers intertwine to strengthen the patient. When a loved one is dying, we reach out a hand to offer reassurance and comfort. In mourning, we console each other by holding hands.

In your loss, did someone hold your hand? Did that simple act comfort you?

Studies show that hand-holding is a powerful way to give comfort and energy to one another. The act of clasping fingers reduces blood pressure and pain. Along with reducing stress, joining hands makes us feel closer to each other. Physically connecting with another human provides many benefits.

Scripture uses the image of God holding our hand to encourage us of his constant closeness. "Yet I am always with you; you hold me by my right hand" (Psalm 73:23).

When we endure heartbreaking trials or the loss of someone dear, we crave hope in the Almighty's presence. Grief from loss may erode our trust in God, leading to questions and doubts, which are part of the grief process. Amid our doubts, questions, and grief, God promises his presence and guidance no matter where we are. We can cling to the image of the Almighty holding our hand.

No matter where we go, God is there. "If I rise on the wings of the dawn, if I settle on the far side of the sea, even there your hand will guide me, your right hand will hold me fast" (Psalm 139:9–10).

Therefore, we are not alone in our sadness because a compassionate God is beside us, providing comfort and care. The image of God holding our hand describes his comfort, strength over fear, and connection. No matter what we feel, God is holding our hands on the grief journey.

"When God holds your hand, he doesn't let go."

—Anonymous

Almighty God,

Please hold my hand in this unknown journey of grief. I need your strength, courage, protection, and guidance. May I experience your comfort. Amen.

Respond: Imagine God holding your hand.

Reflect: Recall times when holding hands gave you a happy feeling.

Read: Isaiah 40:26–31

Journal Prompt: Write a prayer asking God for what you need most today.

Part 3

Doubt in the Storm

Day 12

God Meets Us in Anger

*"How long, L*ORD*? Will you forget me forever?*
How long will you hide your face from me?"

—Psalm 13:1

THOUGHT FOR THE DAY

God listens to our anger.

"GOD IS BIG enough to handle your anger." When I first heard those words during my chaplain training, they made me reconsider my perspective on anger. Previously, I'd thought God would be offended if I expressed my irritation and exasperation or yelled at him with accusations. It seemed disrespectful to rage at God until I found where King David ranted, "How long will you hide your face from me?"

Shortly after, I visited a patient in the hospital who had been hospitalized several times within two months, involving surgery and complications. Her face was flushed, and her words came out sharp with agitation in her voice. She explained her situation and sense of hopelessness about the future. From previous visits, I knew her faith was important to her. As burning tears flowed down her cheeks, she explained her poor health. I allowed her to express her resentment toward God. She needed validation that it was okay to express those emotions. Together, we identified the losses that had resulted in her grief and anger.

I witnessed a sacred moment in that hospital room and a profound change in her demeanor. After expressing anger, she said, "God didn't do this to me, but he will take it and use it in my life." God came into that situation, comforting her and giving her a new perspective.

This patient's story taught me how God meets us when we verbalize our raw negative emotions. Our Heavenly Father is not offended by our raging when we cry out, "It's unfair!" He can deal with our questions and complaints.

The book of Psalms contains songs of praise and psalms of lament, in which the writer pours out bitter feelings with questions of "Why, God?" Each time, words of anger or injustice flow onto the page, soaking the paper. Then the complaint transitions into a petition for God to help. Finally, the psalm ends with words of hope in a faithful God.

When we experience loss, sometimes our sadness turns into anger. We can follow the pattern in the psalms of lament, which starts with expressing our deep, pent-up emotions. Let those emotions cascade like a waterfall, and God will draw near.

Usually, our outlook changes over time, and we realize that God didn't cause pain, loss, or sickness. We notice glimpses of God's goodness in our circumstances, and a fresh trust emerges. God meets us in our angry place.

"I'm glad I was honest with God when I cried out in anger to Him. You will be too."

—Micca Campbell

All-knowing God,

My loss seems so unfair, and sometimes I want to scream. I don't like these feelings, especially when my anger is directed at you. Draw near and meet me in my angry shouts and tears. Amen.

Reflect: In your loss, do you have a sense of injustice?

Respond: Express your anger to God in this time of grief.

Read: Psalm 13

Journal Prompt: Describe what angers, frustrates, and disappoints you about your loss.

Day 13

Winter of the Soul

"Weeping may tarry for the night,
but joy comes with the morning."

—Psalm 30:5 ESV

THOUGHT FOR THE DAY

"Grief is the price we pay for love."
—Queen Elizabeth II

WHEN WILL THIS grief ever end? I asked after my sons had been diagnosed with a rare disease and disabilities. As the days dragged on, I compared my grief to the soul's winter. The howling wind led me to question my sanity. My grief came unexpectedly and uninvited. Life as I knew it disappeared. Despair invaded, and I descended into the black hole of winter. Each day was a constant fight with relentless discouragement.

Like my isolating heartache, many face the loss of a family member, a friend, or a career, divorce, disability, or the devastating bereavement of a dream. Grief is inevitable and universal to all. We all suffer loss, whether it is mental illness, addiction, infertility, rape, the aging process, etc. Loss often brings grief in its wake—a deep, aching sorrow that touches the core of our being. Like the winter season, grief freezes our souls, creates discomfort and distress, and its intensity can overwhelms us.

Jerry Sittser lost his wife, a young daughter, and his mother in a car accident, leaving three children to raise by himself. He mourned and yet simultaneously had to learn to live for his children. Sorrow became a permanent resident in his heart, and a persistent darkness settled in. Sittser decision to enter the darkness of grief had both negative and positive consequences. Negative because he had to face the pain and positive because he went forward toward growth and healing. He grew as he worked on his grief.[1] Through his struggles and pain, he reached his breaking point, which opened him up to a deeper connection with God. He realized God suffered alongside him.

As with the winter season, when trees store nutrients for growth, Sittser grew in experiencing God's grace coming over and around him, providing strength, courage, and hope daily. Nothing could separate him from God's love and Christ's redemptive power, which offers limitless mercy. Sittser explains, "Grace will bring good out of a bad situation; it will take an evil and somehow turn it into something that results in good. That is what God accomplished through the crucifixion."[2]

I also encountered God's grace through my sons' illness. Looking back, I see how divine guidance upheld me and how his strong arms carried me through each day. I have found, "Weeping may tarry for the night, but joy comes with the morning."

"His grief he will not forget; but it will not darken his heart, it will teach him wisdom."

—J. R. R. Tolkien

---

[1] Jerry Sittser, *A Grace Disguised: How the soul grows through loss* (Grand Rapids, Michigan: Zondervan, 2021), 23.
[2] Sittiser, *A Grace Disguised*, 88.

Dear gracious and merciful God,

Help me be willing to enter the pain. Hold me in your compassion and grace. May I see what you are teaching me. Amen.

Reflect: Consider how your grief is like winter of the soul.

Respond: Ask God for grace in your time of loss.

Read: Romans 8:28–39

Journal Prompt: Write about the wisdom you have gained from your loss.

Day 14

Sufficient Grace

"My grace is sufficient for you, for my power is made perfect in weakness."

—2 Corinthians 12:9

THOUGHT FOR THE DAY

God's storehouse of grace has no limit.

IN THE LATE 1800s, Annie Johnson Flint became a prolific poet whose personal struggles profoundly influenced her writing. Orphaned as a child, she was later adopted by a Christian family. In her twenties, she developed severe arthritis, which forced her to retire from teaching and to give up her dream of becoming a concert pianist. Shortly after, both her adoptive parents died. As the disease worsened, it limited her mobility, leaving her dependent on others for care. Despite these physical hardships and pain, Annie's faith in God's goodness and mercy remained unshaken. She persisted in writing poetry, even with her crippled, twisted hands.

Subsequently, Annie's life reflected a powerful testament to God's grace amid frailty. One poem she penned used the metaphor of a storehouse as our stockpile of strength and emotional resilience. God gives us endurance and the necessary resources when our storehouse becomes depleted. The greater the depletion, the greater the grace. When trials increase, God multiples peace. As afflictions pile up, the Almighty adds more mercy. When burdens increase, he gives more stamina. Nick Aufenkamp arranged the poem into music, and it became a beloved hymn, "He Giveth More Grace."

During periods of sadness, many feel a lack of inner resources, experiencing physical exhaustion and a mental fog. Often, bereaved individuals forget what day it is, misplace an object, or feel guilty for not getting over the grief more quickly. Words for prayer don't come, and the grief doesn't vanish.

Similarly, the apostle Paul wrote of a thorn in the flesh that he prayed for God to remove. His suffering persisted, and then God said, "My grace is sufficient for you, for my power is made perfect in weakness" (2 Corinthians 12:9). Instead of relief from the affliction, God's grace enabled Paul to endure.

Like Paul, we can view our grief as a thorn in the flesh that causes anguish, one we wish would disappear. But God's grace is not just a comforting presence; it's a source of strength. Amid our sadness, God's grace replenishes our bare shelves with his power, mercy, peace, and endurance. It comes underneath us, holding us up, empowering us to endure.

Call out to God and seek his grace for your daily needs. Sustaining grace will come.

"[God's] love has no limit; His grace has no measure."

—Annie Flint

Dear God of all grace,

My sorrow drains my reserves and leaves me feeling empty. Replenish my reserves. Provide the strength I need for today. May your grace carry me through and be sufficient. Amen.

Reflect: Remember the times God has supplied your need.

Respond: Thank God for freely giving grace.

Read: 2 Corinthians 12:1–10

Journal Prompt: Describe when your storehouse was barren and how your Heavenly Father provided.

Faith Enables Us

"GOD, the Lord, is my strength; he makes my feet like the deer's;
he makes me tread on my high places."

—Habakkuk 3:19 ESV

THOUGHT FOR THE DAY

Faith looks beyond circumstances.

DO YOU EVER question God when grief overwhelms you?

How can a good God allow this to happen? one woman asked herself after she lost her husband to a brain injury during their first year of marriage. Her grief overcame her and smothered her. Emotions swirled within her, spiraling into a chaotic whirlwind. Well-meaning folks bombarded her with mixed messages, making noise that inhibited her from hearing God.

The Old Testament prophet Habakkuk questioned God, too. He experienced intense sadness from the loss caused by injustice and cruelty around him. He lamented with a broken heart the dire circumstances of his nation and people, wrestling with how to make sense of all that had happened. "How long, LORD, must I call for help, but you do not listen?" (Habakkuk 1:2). God replied to the prophet, "but the righteous shall live by faith" (Habakkuk 2:4 ESV). Habakkuk's eyes had been on the situation rather than on the sustainer of the universe. Despite his complaints, he acknowledged God's ability to provide strength in the midst of adversity and grief.

In the end, Habakkuk didn't need to understand; instead, he could live by faith. He used a metaphor of a deer climbing cliffs to illustrate how faith rises above what can be seen. The powerful legs of deer allow them to escape predators with remarkable speed and agility. At the same time, their tough hooves enable them to traverse even the harshest landscapes. Just as deer are equipped with sure footing to scale rugged terrain, God empowers those who trust in him to face challenges, endure hardships, and believe in his plan—even when the path ahead seems impossible.

Many of us face the grief that besieges us as this young woman whose husband died of a brain injury. She found that quieting herself to read God's Word daily enabled her to listen and trust, and the Scriptures encouraged her to focus on a faithful God. The journey proved challenging, but as her faith grew, it filled her with a strength beyond anything she could imagine.

Faith focuses on God, who is loving, faithful, and sovereign. No matter our circumstances, God will empower us to get through grief.

"Faith is depending on God when you are living in the unknown."

—Jonathan Evans

Sovereign Lord,

You are the giver of life. By the life, death, and resurrection of Christ, you overcame. May my eyes be on you. Empower, enable, and equip me to face the unknown. In Jesus' name, amen.

Reflect: Consider what faith is.

Respond: Find a quiet place to listen to God.

Read: Habakkuk 3

Journal Prompt: What seems impossible for you right now?

Day 16

Questions Remain

*"Now we see things imperfectly, like puzzling reflections
in a mirror, but then we will see everything with perfect clarity.
All that I know now is partial and incomplete."*

—1 Corinthians 13:12 NLT

THOUGHT FOR THE DAY

Someday we will understand the unknowns.

WHY DID THIS *happen?* I questioned this when one of my sons developed a mental illness. I searched for remedies in medical science, consulted the internet to learn, and explored books. I lost part of my son, and I wanted him back! My questions led to sleepless nights where I grappled with the unknowns and cried out in the dark, sometimes with loud wails and other times with silent tears, praying, *Where are you, God?*

In our modern society, we come to expect explanations. When Isaac Newton unlocked many of the universe's mysteries, revealing the unifying force of gravity, he paved the way for people to seek the truth about the world through discovery and testing, using rational thought during the Age of Reason. Since then, we have employed scientific methods and reasoning to find answers and solutions that make sense.

However, some events and losses defy logic, leading us to struggle with unknowns and no explanations, like questions about loss of mental health. We ask, *Why, God?* We are not alone, because this existential question has occupied the minds of theologians and philosophers for centuries and has remained a pressing concern.

In ancient times, Job searched for a reasonable explanation for the tragedies in his life. He lost his children, livestock, and health, and he suffered grief. His friends tried to find answers to Job's pain, but no satisfactory explanation could be found. Eventually, Job abandoned his quest for "why" and trusted God's wisdom. When he surrendered, he found rest.

As with Job, certain unknowns, including losses, lack answers. We can acknowledge these mysteries and categorize them as unknowns. This side of heaven, "We see things imperfectly, like puzzling reflections in a mirror." Nevertheless, someday we will understand fully.

It took me time to trust God and relinquish my son's situation to him. When we surrender our pain to God, he can use it for good, transforming it into something meaningful that shapes us from within. Then our pain becomes purposeful, and it does something in us. It doesn't make everything better, but it makes us better. Christ is the source of our healing, even though the scars remain.

We know that someday our understanding will be complete, he takes ashes and creates beauty.

"My weakness, that is, my quadriplegia, is my greatest asset because it forces me into the arms of Christ every single morning when I get up."

—Joni Eareckson Tada

Heavenly Father,

Grant to us the serenity of mind to accept that which cannot be changed, courage to change that which can be changed, and wisdom to know the one from the other through Jesus Christ our Lord. Amen.[3]

Reflect: What challenges in your life feel beyond your control?

Respond: Make a plan to change what you can.

Read: Job 1–2

Journal Prompt: Write a prayer of surrender to God.

---

[3] This prayer, called the Serenity Prayer, is attributed to Reinhold Niebuhr.

Day 17

God Renews Strength

*"He gives strength to the weary and increases the power
of the weak. . . . but those who hope in the LORD
will renew their strength."*

—Isaiah 40:29–31

THOUGHT FOR THE DAY

God renews our strength.

AFTER MY FATHER died, I functioned in a mental fog, zapped of energy. I noticed little motivation for my job or taking care of my home. Cooking and cleaning seemed like a heavy burden. Each day and every day proved difficult while sadness engulfed me. To add to my feelings, I lost my compass and security when I lost my dad. I needed courage to make it through the day.

Some days, panic weighed on my chest as I got out of bed. Often, I felt like I was scaling a mountain. When my feet hit the floor, I wondered if I could take the next step. One day, I even got lost going home because of fuzzy thinking.

Because of my grief, words didn't come when I tried to pray. All I could do was utter a straightforward prayer without lengthy sentences or elegant words. That supplication went like this: *God, help!* I cried out for strength with that two-word sentence, sometimes hour by hour.

God never failed to give me the courage I needed. Frequently, comfort arrived through a psalm from the Bible or a Christian song on the radio. A friend would call offering encouragement, my boss lessened my job responsibilities, and church members supported me with love, comfort, and prayer. Without fail, comfort came in many forms. Sure enough, strength came.

Undoubtedly, everyone experiences loss differently and in unexpected ways. Have you ever experienced a sense of weakness and fatigue after a loss, particularly a recent one? Ask for what you need with two simple words: *God, help!* When you don't know what you need and don't know what to ask for, reach out by saying, *God, help!*

Throughout your day, carry those basic yet powerful words with you. *God, help!* The Almighty will hear and provide the strength you need. What's more, Scripture promises renewed strength. "He gives strength to the weary and increases the power of the weak. . . . but those who hope in the LORD will renew their strength. They will soar on wings like eagles; they will run and not grow weary, they will walk and not be faint" (Isaiah 40:29-31).

No matter your challenges, trust that God will grant you the strength needed for every hour and every day.

"It is God who arms me with strength
and keeps my way secure."

—Psalm 18:32

God of all strength,

Help! Be my strength when I am depleted, weary, and weak. Please give me courage to face the day and help me take the next step. May I have peace when I sleep. Renew my strength. Through Christ Jesus, amen.

Respond: Thank God for giving strength when needed.

Reflect: How did God enable you to get through yesterday?

Read: Judges 6:11–8:32

Journal Prompt: Write a prayer for what you need. Start with "God, help!"

Season of Suffering

"In my distress, I called to the LORD;
I cried to my God for help.
From his temple, he heard my voice;
my cry came before him, into his ears."

—Psalm 18:6

THOUGHT FOR THE DAY

God hears when we call for help.

"WHY ME, AND why has cancer attacked my body?" Linda asked. As her best friend, I watched as she battled cancer for years, dealing with chemotherapy, pills, hair loss, and countless doctor appointments. She envied her disease-free peers during her dark days while mourning the loss of her health and the loss of all the activities and tasks she used to do. Linda would ask me, "Why me, and why has cancer attacked my body?"

As Linda grappled with her suffering, she came to a profound realization: everyone, without exception, encounters their season of suffering. It could be chronic pain, the death of a loved one, a broken relationship, divorce, disability, or other painful circumstances. These situations lead us to pray, "In my distress, I called to the LORD; I cried to my God for help."

Linda often reminded me, "We all have our own Gethsemane." To clarify, Linda used Gethsemane as a metaphor for a season of suffering. In her word use, she referred to Christ's time in the garden before his arrest and death. Jesus walked with his disciples to the garden of Gethsemane on the Mount of Olives after the Last Supper. In the darkness of the night hour, he wrestled in solemn prayer to the Heavenly Father, knowing crucifixion awaited him. Our Savior knelt in extreme anguish and distress, to the point of sweating drops of blood, while an angel strengthened him. Then Jesus told his disciples, "My soul is overwhelmed with sorrow to the point of death. Stay here and keep watch with me" (Matthew 26:38). The garden was a time of suffering as Christ bore the burden of death on a cross.

When we grieve a loss whether health or another kind of loss, we experience deep emotional anguish. Our sorrow weighs heavily on us, draining our strength like an olive press extracting oil. The original meaning of Gethsemane is "oil press." In such times, we may feel as though we are in our own season of suffering—our personal Gethsemane. But we are not alone in our grief, for Christ comforts and empathizes with us.

When overwhelmed by our circumstances, we can remember that God knows exactly how we are feeling. We have the privilege of calling out to God for grace in our time of need. God hears our cries and will respond by giving us the strength and support we need.

"Do not apologize for crying. Without this emotion, we are only robots."

—Elizabeth Gilbert

Dear Jesus,

As you received strength in the garden, strengthen me in my grief. My loss saddens my heart to the point of anguish. I call out to you. Hear my cries of distress and lift me up. In your name, amen.

Reflect: Consider Jesus' sorrow in the garden before his crucifixion.

Respond: In your distress, cry out to God for help.

Read: Psalm 18:6–20

Journal Prompt: What is your personal Gethsemane?

Part 4

Beginning to Breathe Again

God Is Near the Brokenhearted

"The LORD is close to the brokenhearted
and saves those who are crushed in spirit."

—Psalm 34:18

THOUGHT FOR THE DAY

God mends our brokenness.

WHEN MY SEVENTEEN-YEAR-OLD son lost his father to cancer, I worried about and wondered how to help him process his grief. After conducting some research, I discovered the Children's Bereavement Center, which offers sessions specifically for teenagers. My son gained some needed skills to navigate through many rough months after his dad died.

One of the tools the Center used was a mural painted on a long wall with a series of hearts to depict the grief journey. The first painting begins with a plain white heart encircled by dark clouds to represent how grief starts, and the second heart turns a completely dark gray. The following image depicts a black heart with a wide crack down the middle, symbolizing the darkness and brokenness associated with grief. In the following image, the gloom fades, and the heart turns lighter while a tiny seed drifts into the crack. Finally, light surrounds the last heart, the crack grows smaller, and delicate flowers grow from the crevice.[4]

This mural shows the transformation from a broken heart to a mended heart. Hope comes, mending begins, and something beautiful grows out of the grief.

An example of a broken heart in Scripture is Hannah, who was barren. To compound her grief, her husband's second wife, who had several children, taunted her continually. While distressed and discouraged, she journeyed with her family to the tabernacle. There she poured out her sorrow. "Hannah was in deep anguish, crying bitterly as she prayed to the LORD" (1 Samuel 1:10 NLT). The Almighty met Hannah in tears and heard her prayers by sending the priest, Eli, to reassure her. Hannah left strengthened with hope; the following year, she had a child.

Much like Hannah, who ached, our souls ache from grief. When we lose someone we deeply care about or experience any type of profound loss, the hole in our lives can seem like a deep fissure. As we cry out to a compassionate God, he shows up alongside and is near in our sadness. Comfort, strength, and hope come in the form of a sunrise, new blooms in spring, Scripture promises, caring friends, or inspiring music. Through the Holy Spirit, our hearts heal. With time, we notice something good emerging from our brokenness.

"There is a sacredness in tears. They are the messengers of overwhelming grief, of deep contrition, and of unspeakable love."

—Washington Irving

---

[4] Judy Pelikan, *The Heart's Journey* (New York: Abbeville Press 1996).

Dear Divine Mender,

Be my refuge in the pain of grief. Be my healer in times of brokenness. Take the wounds left from my loss and transform them into something beautiful you can use. Amen.

Reflect: Reflect on where your heart is in the grief journey. Do black clouds surround your heart? Does your heart have a gaping crack down the middle? Are you seeing light?

Respond: Picture God mending your heart and flowers growing from the cracks.

Read: 1 Samuel 1

Journal Prompt: What are the cracks in your heart from your loss?

Day 20

Healing Friends

"Praise be to the Lord, to God our Savior,
who daily bears our burdens."

—Psalm 68:19

THOUGHT FOR THE DAY

God carries our burdens
and sends others to help.

I PLANNED MY life, intending to marry after college and then have children, which I did. However, life took an unexpected plot twist when I birthed two sons with a rare disease and multiple disabilities. Besides all the physical demands on me, their disease impacted me emotionally, and I didn't have the tools to navigate my emotions. Grief became my constant companion when I went to bed at night and every turn. When I saw other typical children, I hurt for my sons. I noticed development lags and became fearful. I couldn't run from it. I grieved on the first day of kindergarten because my sons were placed in exceptional education. I grieved when other children played games, attended parties, and had friends.

To compound my heartache, few listened with empathy. My peers were busy with their families and unable to comprehend my sorrow. Some church folks judged me, and others minimized my concerns. It wasn't until I met other parents with special needs children who became my comforting friends. They heard me out, were empathetic, and didn't judge me or look for what I did wrong to have two children with special needs. They exemplified the verse of Galatians 6:2: "Carry each other's burdens." Having someone walking alongside me eased my burden and helped me persevere.

Kenneth C. Haugk, a pastor and clinical psychologist, introduced the concept of "healing friends." During his wife's prolonged battle with cancer, he gained valuable insights into the needs of grieving individuals. This experience inspired him to write books, provide counseling, and establish Stephen Ministries. The ministry trains people to support others during loss, crisis, or significant life challenges, offering one-on-one care, empathy, and the gift of walking alongside others. These caregivers show Christ's love and compassion, helping those in need by carrying each other's struggles.

Similarly, a story of healing takes place in Mark 12. While Jesus taught in a house, four friends brought a paralyzed man to him, yet access to Jesus was impossible because of the crowded home. In order to help their friend, they dug a hole through the roof and lowered the mat to Christ, making it possible for the man to be close to the Teacher. Not only did Jesus forgive the man's sins, but he also healed him. This man's healing started with his friends.

I knew God bore my burdens daily, and he did this by sending healing friends. Others gave me comfort by sharing my grief and listening with empathy. God used "healing friends" to begin the mending. I needed a sounding board, understanding, and acceptance. With those gifts from friends, I started to heal and move forward.

God uses the presence of others to lead us to healing.

*"Part of the healing process is sharing
with other people who care."*

—Jerry Cantrell

Dear Jesus,

Bring caring friends into my life. Help me become a better friend to others in need. Amen.

Reflect: If you have caring friends, who are your "healing friends?"

Respond: Ask God to provide companions during your time of loss.

Read: Mark 2:1–12

Journal Prompt: Allow Jesus to be one of your healing friends, tell him about your grief.

Day 21

Beyond Our Endurance

"We were under great pressure, far beyond our ability to endure, so that we despaired of life itself."

—2 Corinthians 1:8

IN THE GRIEF group Carol trembled when she said, "This grief is too much; it is more than I can bear!" I led a monthly grief group that Carol attended. She lost her son to a progressive disease in March and then her husband to cancer in December. As she clenched a tissue, she confessed, "I never had time to grieve for my son because I was taking care of my ill husband."

"Carol, this is huge! Every loss matters and deserves to be honored," I said as I ached with her. In the following weeks, she committed herself to the work of grieving, showing up to the grief group like clockwork. Slowly, Carol opened up, sharing her feelings and eventually bringing glossy photos to celebrate cherished memories of her son and husband. She listened to others' stories and offered them comforting hugs. "I'm so grateful for this group," she told us one day.

Now a year later, Carol connects with other widows, checks on sick neighbors, and attends Bible study while encouraging others to be grateful. She walked the path of what psychologists call compound grief, one loss overlapping another like waves, not having time to catch her breath. Her emotions of grief for each loss merged, becoming more intense and prolonged.

Her journey mirrors that of Naomi from the Old Testament book of Ruth. Naomi experienced the tragedy of three family losses: her husband died, and then both her sons died while she lived in a foreign country. In misery, she returned to Bethlehem, her hometown, with her daughter-in-law, Ruth. Overwhelmed with the sharpness of her grief, Naomi asked to be called Mara, a name that means "bitter." Surrounded by her hometown community and her faithful daughter-in-law, she began to heal by embracing her faith and guiding Ruth.

In God's redemptive plan, Ruth remarries and has a son. Naomi's joyful laughter returns when she embraces her grandson, Obed. He becomes the grandfather of King David. From this line comes Jesus, the promised Messiah.

Sometimes, we feel hopeless under the weight of grief, which can be "far beyond our ability to endure," as the apostle Paul felt when he wrote 2 Corinthians 1:8. He placed his sole trust in God, which led to courage and strength. God's grace enabled Paul to bear the suffering. When the grief you experience exceeds your endurance, depend on the Almighty God to carry you through. God will give you what you need when you ask.

"Faith may want answers, but somehow it is able
to survive without them."

—Carolyn Custis James

Dear redemptive God,

You know my strength fails, and it seems like all the sadness is too much for me. Please help me get through this. Lift me in your everlasting arms, give me what I need, and surround me with your love. Amen.

Reflect: Do you have compound grief? If so, what?

Respond: Be gentle with yourself.

Read: Ruth 1–4

Journal Prompt: Describe ways to care for yourself during grief.

Day 22

Gratitude amid Grief

"Rejoice always, pray continually,
give thanks in all circumstances;
for this is God's will for you in Christ Jesus."

—1 Thessalonians 5:16–18

THOUGHT FOR THE DAY

Gratitude can be an act of faith.

"LOOK AT THE good stuff. Reflect on the beautiful memories. Be grateful," Brownie said in a shaky but firm tone. What she said surprised me because she lost her beloved to cancer during COVID-19 and unfortunately, she could not be with him when he died. She described her husband as her partner, spiritual companion, fellow traveler, mentor, and business partner. Not being able to say goodbye complicated her grief. The unusual and tragic circumstances seemed to suffocate her at first. All who knew Brownie grieved for her. We also mourned his loss because we knew her husband from our Bible study.

As a way to work through her grief, Brownie decided to help others. She helped me start a grief group in our neighborhood. We spent a significant part of the grief class acknowledging and validating emotions that accompany loss, such as sadness, guilt, anger, fear, denial, loneliness, hopelessness, and emptiness. Together, we viewed grief as a journey in the wilderness. During the group meetings, Brownie shared how she would cry and journal in the privacy of her home. However, she said little else about her grief for a long time.

Then, at the seventh meeting, Brownie challenged the attendees with tears running down her cheeks, saying, "Be grateful." Of all people, Brownie could have been bitter, but she encouraged the group to express thankfulness. She said, "Once you are in a state of gratitude, you begin to move forward on the grief journey. Thankfulness gets you over the hump."

Jesus gave thanks in all circumstances at the Last Supper. He took bread, gave thanks, broke it, and gave it to the disciples when he knew the crucifixion awaited him (Luke 22:19). Christ looked ahead to the redemption found in the cross and how this death would allow people to restore their relationship with God.

Expressing gratitude changes our focus and can be an antidote for feelings of hopelessness and despair. Research highlights the benefits of gratitude and how it improves physical and emotional health. Besides improving our attitude, thankfulness also includes a spiritual component, allowing us to notice signs of God working in everyday events. We look beyond ourselves. With a change in focus, we become more aware of God's grace and goodness in our lives.

When we are grieving, gratitude can be an act of faith. As the apostle Paul charged the early church, "Rejoice always ... give thanks in all circumstances."

"Say not in grief 'he is no more' but live in thankfulness that he was."

—MyGriefAssist

Dear good and gracious God,

Thank you for your surpassing love in sending Jesus to redeem me. Please help me to be more grateful in all circumstances and in my grief. Thank you for all you have given me—friends, family, and, most of all, you. Amen.

Reflect: Who has shown you kindness?

Respond: Start a Gratitude List.

Read: Psalm 100

Journal Prompt: Write five things for which you are grateful.

Day 23

Loss of Future Dreams

"But you, God, see the trouble of the afflicted;
you consider their grief and take it in hand.
The victims commit themselves to you;
you are the helper of the fatherless."

—Psalm 10:14

THOUGHT FOR THE DAY

God knows and cares about
our dreams.

"THERE IS SO much I wanted to do with him. Dad didn't even get to see my new house," Zack said. At thirty-three years old, Zack lost his father unexpectedly to a heart attack. His father seemed healthy, showing no warning signs of illness. The shock of his passing left Zack drifting in disbelief, and as the reality settled in, a deep sadness and regret engulfed him. Newly married and established in his career, Zack had purchased his first home just days before his father's death. Choking on his words, he said, "Dad won't be able to visit."

Six months prior, my family joined in celebrating Zack's wedding, where his father played catch with him before the ceremony and later delivered a moving, funny speech at the reception. Life looked hopeful, with many joys ahead.

Zack grieved the absence of his father and the future he'd imagined experiencing with the man in his life he loved most. He mourned his dad's absence for life's milestones—the chance for him to hold his future child or join in family Christmases. With death came a double loss—shattered dreams.

With the death of a loved one, we experience and mourn a tangible loss. Yet our hopes and aspirations are intangible because they reside in our heads and hearts. No one offers us condolences for the unfulfilled hopes while we silently lament this other unexpected layer of grief. Dreams are delicate vessels, holding our wishes, hopes, and fantasies. But this fragile container, a clay jar, can crash to the ground instantly, shattering with a piercing sound into countless pieces. All our aspirations, desires, and plans spill out, leaving only shards scattered in their place.

Nevertheless, our Heavenly Father collects the fragments of our lost dreams, meets our brokenness with his comforting embrace, binds up the wounds, and heals. God observes the depth of our lost hopes and meets us there. We have a promise from "the Father of compassion and the God of all comfort, who comforts us in all our troubles" (2 Corinthians 1:3–4). In time, God will add new dreams.

Zack's earthly father may no longer be with him, yet God remains ever near to those without a father. He comforts us in our sorrow, and takes on the role of a loving Father to the fatherless. As Scripture reminds us: *"But you, God, see the trouble of the afflicted; you consider their grief and take it in hand. The victims commit themselves to you; you are the helper of the fatherless."*

"There is no expiration date on the love between a father and his child."

—Jennifer Williamson

Dear Heavenly Father,

Hallowed be your name, your kingdom come, your will be done, on earth as in heaven. Give us today our daily bread. Forgive us our sins, as we forgive those who sin against us. Lead us not into temptation: But deliver us from evil. For the kingdom, the power, and the glory are yours: Now and forever. Amen.

Reflect: How has God comforted you?

Respond: Ask God to come into your brokenness.

Read: 2 Corinthians 1:2–11

Journal Prompt: Tell about the dreams that were shattered in the wake of your loss.

Day 24

Roller Coaster of Emotions

"The LORD is my rock, my fortress and my deliverer;
my God is my rock, in whom I take refuge."

—Psalm 18:2

THOUGHT FOR THE DAY

We can depend on God, who is our rock.

HAVE YOU EVER felt that your emotions resemble riding a roller coaster? Grief often seems like a roller coaster, plummeting down at the speed of light. I live in a city with two world-renowned theme parks, SeaWorld and Fiesta Texas. Both boast of roller coasters that tower above the horizon and try to outdo each other with steep inclines, swift drops, sudden twists, and changes in direction and speed. Adrenaline draws people worldwide.

However, fun rides are their choice, but loss can bring a roller coaster of emotions for some. I write for a pregnancy loss group, which is a safe place for mothers who have lost babies in utero, had a stillborn baby, or experienced an infant death. These mothers share how their emotions fluctuate, and they wonder if God is with them one moment and then trust God the next. They mourn, and they stagger, reeling from the expectations of others who minimize their loss, which causes them to feel isolated. They commonly describe grief as a journey of dramatic downs and unpredictable turns. One day they're celebrating being pregnant with dreams of holding their baby, and then the next day, they're mourning a miscarriage or infant loss. They battle jealousy when they see other moms with children.

Our society often fails to acknowledge miscarriages and other kinds of losses, such as infertility, divorce or loss of a career. Typical clichés are blurted out, such as "Get over it," making those who experience loss cringe with guilt. Consequently, they ride an emotional roller coaster, twists and turns, ups and downs of emotions.

However, thankfully, we don't stand alone; many of the writers of the psalms capture a spectrum of emotions, giving validity to emotional turbulence. David, who later became king of Israel, experienced emotional peaks and valleys. Yet, he sang a song of the Lord's deliverance from the hand of all his enemies. He sang, "The Lord is my rock, my fortress and my deliverer." Through all the battles, he clung to the truth that God was his rock. The metaphor of a rock conveys God's unchanging character and strength, reminding us of his power, which transcended David's peaks and valleys. God's character transcended David's fears, sorrow, and anger.

Like David, we can rely on a God who remains steadfast amid the ever-changing emotions that come with losing someone dear or experiencing a non-death loss. Our Creator, unwavering and firm, serves as a solid foundation. David declared, "The Lord is my rock." God always remains present to support us.

When your feelings vacillate, run to the Lord, asking him to steady you. Peace and confidence come when we look to God as our rock.

"Grief is an emotional rollercoaster. You will have your ups and downs and moments of terror and brief moments of peace. You can only go as fast as the ride will take you. Just remember: It will end and you will be okay."

—Kate McGahan

Dear God, my rock,

I need you to steady me and be my stable foundation when I have emotional swings. Please help me trust you and cling to you as my deliverer. Support me, and let me lean on you. Amen.

Reflect: Do you see God as strong?

Respond: When emotions fluctuate, visualize God as your rock.

Read: Psalm 18

Journal Prompt: Describe the variability of your emotions this week.

Day 25

In Need of Mercy

*"Have mercy on me, L*ORD*, for I am faint; heal me, L*ORD*,*
for my bones are in agony. My soul is in deep anguish.
*How long, L*ORD*, how long?"*

—Psalm 6:2–3

THOUGHT FOR THE DAY

The throne of grace is open.

"ANOTHER WAVE OF grief knocked me down," I said to my husband. "This one caught me by surprise." It was a milestone birthday for my son, who has multiple health problems, including needing a liver transplant. Sometimes, I am okay, while other days, deep sadness hits. "Why, God? It's not fair!" I journal feelings and earnest prayers. Then I shed tears.

Likewise, non-death losses can arouse grief akin to losing a loved one. Waves of grief crash over us, pulling us under and taking our breath away. Each wave eventually passes, allowing us to surface for air, only to be met by another. Over time, the swells grow less frequent and less intense. Our fear of another wave lessens, and we know we will rise to the surface again.

C.S. Lewis described grief as having your leg amputated. Although the wound may heal, the leg never grows back. The absence of a loved one or another loss will forever remain in our hearts and lives, bearing evidence of loss and resilience.

Our plea is, "Have mercy on me, Lord, for I am faint." We ask, "How long, Lord, how long?" In those moments of crying out to God, he meets us in our anguish, has mercy, and provides what we need. In my experience, the Lord always answers the prayer "Have mercy on me."

The Gospels recount numerous instances of suffering individuals pleading for mercy: a blind man (Luke 18:38), two others likewise blind (Matthew 20:30), a Gentile mother whose child is demon-afflicted (Matthew 15:22), and a father whose son suffers seizures (Matthew 17:15). They all cried out, "Lord, have mercy." For each one, Jesus stopped, listened, and met their need. One account tells of a tax collector who donated to the temple. He grieved over his sins and pleaded for God's mercy, and the Lord forgave him (Luke 18:9–14).

When we approach God humbly and seek forgiveness, he hears our prayers and forgives us. When a wave of grief comes, we can pray, "Have mercy on me!" The Lord, who loves us and is compassionate, will meet us and give us what is needed: a listening friend, a Scripture, a song, or something else.

Over time, the waves of sorrow subside somewhat and grief softens, even though our loss is permanent. We adjust with God's grace. Hope starts to sprout, like the first shoot of a flower in spring. Memories begin to bring smiles.

"God's mercy is so great that you may sooner drain the sea of its water, or deprive the sun of its light, or make space too narrow, then diminish the great mercy of God."

—Charles Spurgeon

God of Mercy,

*Hear my prayer because I need you to meet me in this grief.
Forgive me and bring hope when I am weak. Amen.*

Reflect: Think on God's mercy and forgiveness.

Respond: When a rush of grief knocks you over, ask God for help.

Read: Luke 18

Journal Prompt: Describe your need for mercy at this moment.

Guilt Steals Our Peace

"Peace I leave with you; my peace I give you.
I do not give to you as the world gives.
Do not let your hearts be troubled and do not be afraid."

—John 14:27

"WHAT IF I'D taken her for a second opinion? What if she'd gotten an alternative treatment? Maybe she would be alive." My friend shared with me that her sister-in-law passed away from cancer at a young age.

How often do we blame ourselves for decisions we make when a loved one is ill or when we experience another kind of loss? We examine what we've done, mulling it over and over. All the while, we regret not having done more.

Indeed, guilt—a persistent and gnawing feeling in our gut—is a regular part of grieving. We lament missed opportunities or wonder if we could have changed the outcome. Often we wish we could retract the words we have said. Guilt says, "If only." While self-blame can be a common emotion, it may not always be logical.

In addition, guilt can lead us to have unrealistic expectations about circumstances we can't change.

A well-known grief counselor, Dr. Alan Wolflet, says, "Guilt, regret, and self-blame are natural feelings after the death of someone loved."[5] He says the keys include being compassionate toward ourselves and having a conversation about our feelings. As we openly and honestly explore guilt with empathic listeners, we come to understand the limits of our responsibility and, upon review, realize that no one is perfect.

Besides exploring our feelings with a nonjudgmental friend, we can talk to the Lord. When Christ walked the earth, he didn't heal everyone who needed healing. Jesus didn't explain it then, but he promised to give us peace, saying, "Peace I leave with you; my peace I give you. I do not give to you as the world gives."

The throne room of heaven is open to us, where we can lay down our regrets and ask for forgiveness if needed. "Let us then approach God's throne of grace with confidence, so that we may receive mercy and find grace to help us in our time of need" (Hebrews 4:16). As we pray, comfort and peace come.

"Guilt is perhaps the most painful companion to death."

—Elisabeth Kubler-Ross

Forgiving God,

You know, I wish things had played out differently, and I wish I had done more or said something else. Forgive me. Please help me let go of the "what ifs" and "should haves." Help me forgive myself. I place my guilt at the foot of the cross. In Jesus' name, amen.

---

[5] Alan D. Wolfelt, *Understanding Your Grief: Ten essential touchstones for finding hope and healing your heart* (Fort Collins, Colorado: Companion Press 2021), 79.

Reflect: Consider the positive things you did.

Respond: Share your guilt with a nonjudgmental friend.

Read: Psalm 103:1–18

Journal Prompt: Write a list of "what ifs" on a separate paper. Ask God to forgive you if needed and commit them to God, then tear up the list.

Part 5

First Lights of Healing

Day 27

God Is Our Strength

"God is our refuge and strength,
an ever-present help in trouble."

—Psalm 46:1

THOUGHT FOR THE DAY

God is present in your situation.

HAVE YOU EVER felt like your whole world crumbled beneath you after losing someone you loved or something you cherished? I lost my footing and thought I would sink into an abyss when my best friend, Margie, passed. Our friendship spanned forty years, sharing each other's lives throughout that entire time. When she died, I panicked with what seemed like nonstop sobbing. I told my husband, "Margie held my history, dreams, challenges, and successes. She carried me through many hard days and celebrated when I married you." Her presence radiated empathy, ever ready to listen and uplift.

Growing up in South Florida on the coast, builders constructed homes by laying the foundation on pilings, long concrete poles with steel rods inside that were drilled deep into the sandy soil. The pilings provided stability to the substructure. Homes without them underneath gradually sank. Pilings support high-rise condominiums, withstanding violent hurricanes and erosion from flooding. When Maggie died, I lost a part of me and part of my foundation.

I turned to the Scriptures to gain strength, finding comfort in Psalm 46:1: "God is our refuge and strength, an ever-present help in trouble." I began to depend on God more, allowing him to be the sturdy pillar under me. Courage came as I learned to rely on my Heavenly Father.

Another person who related to Psalm 46 is Martin Luther, the reformer of the 1500s. He penned a well-known hymn, "A Mighty Fortress Is Our God." He described God as a strong fortification, a helper, and a defensive wall amid floods of ongoing struggles and hardships. Luther confronted many obstacles in his lifetime: the Black Plague, losing a child, religious controversies, and death threats. He trusted God to be his mighty bastion from enemies, Christ to give victory over all the ills of this human life, and the Holy Spirit to be always present with him.

Grieving takes time. Our values change, we reluctantly adjust, and we learn to find fortitude in knowing we have a God who is always present in every trouble, a God who is our foundation. Even in the pain of losing someone so dear, I clung to God's promise, repeating it again and again: "Never will I leave you; never will I forsake you" (Hebrews 13:5).

"God is a God of the present. God is always in the moment, be that moment hard or easy, joyful or painful."

—Henri Nouwen

Almighty God,

I come needing refuge and strength. Please give me the bravery to face each day, and may I experience your presence. In the name of the Father, Son, and Holy Spirit, amen.

Reflect: When do you sense God?

Respond: Look up the words to "A Mighty Fortress Is Our God."

Read: Psalm 46

Journal Prompt: Tell how you are learning to let God be your strength.

Day 28

God Sees You

*"She gave this name to the LORD, who spoke to her:
'You are the God who sees me,' for she said,
'I have now seen the One who sees me.'"*

—Genesis 16:13

THOUGHT FOR THE DAY

God sees you.

"WHEN I LOST my sister to cancer, I lost my best friend," Ann said to me when we visited over coffee. Even as her friend, I couldn't fully grasp the depth of her loss. Losing a sibling can be like losing a part of yourself, your history, and your identity. My friend and her sister cherished their weekly lunches and shared looking in on their parents. Ann experienced a sense of abandonment when her only sibling died.

When Ann learned of her sister's diagnosis of invasive brain cancer, she quit her job. My friend took full responsibility for managing her sibling's medical oversight, all without a single complaint. Ann's role as a caregiver left her perpetually exhausted and made her more challenged by the demands of her young family.

Ann's world crashed in around her when her sister died within a year, leaving a hole like a deep cavern that ached for her sister's companionship. Ann seemed unmotivated and lacked energy, spending time slumped on the couch, watching TV show reruns. She endured deep emotional pain, maybe even trauma, from the loss of someone she held so dear.

The Scriptures describe a woman who experienced abandonment by those she trusted. Hagar, an Egyptian servant girl, traveled to a foreign land to serve her master, Sarai, Abram's wife. Despite their wealth, Sarai's husband, Abram, had no heir. Although God had promised Abram a descendant, Sarai remained barren. Determined to secure an heir for her husband, Sarai devised a plan to use Hagar as a means to an end. Hagar conceived Abram's child, but tension arose between the women. Sarai mistreated her servant, and thus Hagar fled.

Hagar reached a low point in the desert, pregnant, without a home or family. An angel appeared to the runaway, reassuring and instructing her to return to Sarai. God saw and heard Hagar and promised her a son. She could stand tall, knowing the Lord was by her side. Afterward, Hagar used a name for God: "You are the God who sees me."

When we lose a close loved one, we can experience a sense of abandonment, similar to trauma. At those times, we can draw encouragement from the story of Hagar. Like Hagar, God saw Ann's solitude, and comfort came from her family, church members, and friends. Gradually, Ann drew strength from studying the Scriptures, coupled with prayer. The sparkle in her eyes reappeared, and her energy returned with renewed motivation.

"There is sacredness in tears. They are not the mark of weakness, but of power. They are the messengers of overwhelming grief, of deep contrition, and of unspeakable love."

—Washington Irving

Dear all-seeing God,

Thank you for seeing me. Walk beside me to comfort me, calm down my anxiety, and reassure my lonely heart. Please bring others to help fill the gap. Amen.

Reflect: When have you felt abandoned?

Respond: Plan to read Scripture daily.

Read: Genesis 16

Journal Prompt: How have you experienced God's intervention when you felt alone?

Day 29

Peace Beyond Understanding

"Do not be anxious about anything, but in every situation,
by prayer and petition, with thanksgiving, present your requests
to God. And the peace of God, which transcends all understanding,
will guard your hearts and minds in Christ Jesus."

—Philippians 4:6–7

THOUGHT FOR THE DAY

God calms our hearts.

"CHRISTMAS WILL FOREVER be different. Why didn't God stop this?" Beverly asked after she lost her son. Jason had PTSD after two tours in Iraq, struggled with health problems caused by a disease, and later contracted COVID-19. Stress built up, and the ultimate hardship came when he needed to isolate himself from his family during COVID-19. His loved ones found him, and authorities determined his death a suicide.

Initially, Beverly responded with, *Why?* Then she blamed herself, *What could I have done differently?* Gripped with fear, she wondered if she would see Jason in heaven. Her thoughts whirled, and her emotions were like an angry sea.

An example of raging emotions and conflict is the story of a small fishing boat on the Sea of Galilee tossed in a fierce gale. Jesus' followers crouched in the boat as violent gusts and soaring waves battered the ship, threatening to break it apart while water poured in. Fear and anxiety filled the disciples as they weathered the storm. Meanwhile, Jesus slept undisturbed at the bottom of the vessel. In their panic, the disciples shouted to Jesus to wake up. Jesus spoke to the storm. The winds stopped, and the waters calmed. However, it wasn't until they asked the Savior to calm the sea that the storm became still, fears subsided, and their trust in Jesus grew (Matthew 8:23-27).

Beverly worked through her thoughts by reviewing the Scriptures, which enabled her to say, *God wasn't to blame*. Over time, she came to terms with the guilt. Then she was able to forgive herself. "Only God," she said, "can provide comfort after a suicide." Beverly prayed about her concerns, entrusting her pain to the Lord. The healing process began.

She found solace in talking to friends, who allowed her to work through her feelings. Also, her experience with Adult Children of Alcoholics and Dysfunctional Families provided her with strategies to cope.

Beverly's journey stretched long, with Christmases remaining sad, yet she turned to a merciful Lord with petitions and thanksgiving. Peace settled over her as she immersed herself in Scripture. "God and friends got me through," Beverly acknowledged. The assurance came that Jason rested safely in Jesus' arms. Her heart holds peace that "transcends understanding" for Jesus has stepped in and calmed her storm.

"Sadness does not sink a person; it is the energy a person spends trying to avoid sadness that does that."

—Barbara Brown Taylor

Dear Jesus,

Come into my chaos, calm the storm, and bring peace. Join me, like you did the disciples. Let the storm within me subside, and comfort me in my grief. In Jesus' name, amen.

Reflect: When have you experienced peace?

Respond: Give God your anxieties.

Read: Mark 4:35–41

Journal Prompt: Describe the storm you felt when you had a loss.

Day 30

Inwardly Renewed

"He makes me lie down in green pastures,
he leads me beside quiet waters, he refreshes my soul.
He guides me along the right paths for his name's sake."

—Psalm 23:2–3

> ### THOUGHT FOR THE DAY
>
> God renews our strength.

DETERMINED TO RETURN to work the week after my father passed away, I assured myself, *I can handle this grief—after all, I'm a chaplain.* On my next overnight shift, a call came in the middle of the night: a family needed a chaplain. When I arrived, the patient had already passed. All the family gathered around their father's bedside while I prayed and gave pastoral care. Even though their father endured a prolonged illness, his death visibly shook them. After I prayed with the family, I worked on paperwork in the living room. Suddenly, I panicked, and all the strength drained out of my body, remembering the shock I felt when Dad died. I thought, *This death is so much like his. It's only been a little over a week since he died.*

I expected to bounce back from my father's death, but my body didn't cooperate. I felt like a limp rag with no energy and wondered how I would drive home. To this day, I don't understand how I completed the documentation and arrived home. Emotionally drained, I ached deep in my chest, and even the simplest tasks felt exhausting. My thoughts swirled as I whispered, "I need God to nurture me." My boss lightened my workload and reminded me to be gentle with myself; her kindness offered comfort in my time of loss.

The story of Elijah helped me permit myself to slow down. The prophet spent enormous energy when he challenged 450 priests of Baal. He prayed for rain, outran a chariot, and slew the pagan prophets. God used him powerfully, but shortly after, Elijah grew discouraged and wished to die. Fearing a death threat from the queen, he ventured into the wilderness, far from everything, and slept. An angel brought Elijah bread and water while he rested. God granted respite and nourishment to strengthen him in the wilderness before his next assignment (1 Kings 19:3-8).

If God provided a time-out and sustenance to Elijah, then maybe God desires that for us. I thought of this verse: "He makes me lie down in green pastures, he leads me beside quiet waters, he refreshes my soul."

After a loss we need nurture and time to recover emotionally, physically and spiritually. When we allow ourselves time to grieve, we open up space for spiritual renewal. God will refresh us when we pray, read the Scriptures, and meditate. Sacred music often lifts our spirits, just as quiet walks in nature do. Expect less of yourself, be gentle with yourself and allow time to be inwardly renewed.

"By finding time to rest, we can overcome our fears, renew our trust in Him, and reignite ourselves for the spiritual journeys ahead."

—e3 Partners

Loving Lord,

You are aware of how tired and depleted I am. Help me slow down, give me rest, and encourage me. Renew my spirit. Amen.

Reflect: Think about what refreshes you.

Respond: Decide to give up one or more tasks.

Read: 1 Kings 18–19

Journal Prompt: Describe how you felt when you rested.

Day 31

A Safe Place

"Have mercy on me, my God, have mercy on me,
for in you I take refuge. I will take refuge in the shadow
of your wings until the disaster has passed."

—Psalm 57:1

"I DON'T KNOW how to move forward after losing my dad. He was my security," she said. Olivia depended on her dad to guide and support her with decisions and be her confidant. Now she experienced a physical ache in her chest when the fear of life without him gripped her. Even with her own family—a husband and children—her father was her anchor. When she was a single mom, she leaned on him.

Losing a loved one or experiencing another kind of loss often threatens a person's sense of security. The world, once familiar, now seems different, causing us to relearn it. Security and safety rank among humanity's most fundamental needs. According to Maslow's hierarchy of needs, security ranks second on the pyramid, following physical needs. God understands our need to feel protected and gives us promises in Scripture.

One example given in God's Word is the image of the "shadow of your wings." This metaphor creates a visual picture of God as sheltering, like a mother bird protecting her vulnerable chicks beneath her wings, offering unconditional guidance, safety, and care. An ancient hymn writer penned, "Keep me as the apple of your eye; hide me in the shadow of your wings" (Psalm 17:8). As a magnificent eagle spreads its mighty wings to protect hatchlings from predators, storms, and the sun's heat, God guards us from harm.

Furthermore, Jesus used the metaphor of a mother hen gathering her chicks to protect them. He longed to shelter his people under his wings. The mother hen's fierce, selfless instincts offer refuge despite a significant personal cost, embodying protective love. Jesus desires for us to find strength in him through life's difficulties.

Similarly, God invites us into his presence as a sanctuary, a place of peace and refuge. When fear overwhelmed her, Olivia turned to God as her sanctuary, praying to her Heavenly Father for protection and guidance. More than anything, she yearned to rest and experience the comfort under his wings. God became her best friend. She often envisioned herself secure under the shelter of his wings and trust grew in Olivia's heart.

"When things fall apart, the broken pieces
allow all sorts of things to enter, and one of them
is the presence of God."

—Shauna Niequist

Lord Jesus Christ,

You stretched out your arms of love on the hardwood of the cross that everyone might come within the reach of your saving embrace. Amen. (The Book of Common Prayer)

Reflect: Envision yourself in the sanctuary of his presence, sheltered by his wings.

Respond: Ask God to help you trust when insecurity comes.

Read: Psalm 91

Journal Prompt: Do you see God as a protector? Explain why or why not.

Day 32

Jesus Offers Peace

"On the evening of that first day of the week, when the disciples were together, with the doors locked for fear of the Jewish leaders, Jesus came and stood among them and said, 'Peace be with you!'"

—John 20:19

THOUGHT FOR THE DAY

Jesus offers peace and reassurance.

A MASS SCHOOL shooting took place in a rural, close-knit farming town about a hundred miles from San Antonio. For days, headlines about the loss of children and adults saturated the news. We all staggered with painful grief and couldn't shake our shock. The small town and the surrounding areas mourned collectively. Community grief occurs when a society or nation faces a tragedy or natural disaster.

Saddened and helpless, I prayed for those affected by the attack. Then, a request came for chaplains to provide pastoral care for the hospital staff who treated the children and teachers in the massacre. Thankful for the opportunity to help, I drove two hours there and prayed for words.

When I arrived, I listened with empathy to the nurses' stories, holding their pain and words in my heart. One told of embracing a dying child, overwhelmed with helplessness. Another recounted weeping parents in the waiting area, anxiously awaiting news of their child's survival. Some were parents themselves. "What will I tell my kids? I can't tell them I can keep them safe?" said a nurse of two elementary school children. Survivor's guilt and fear consumed another. Most staff members had connections with one or more of the bereaved families. I said little because they needed listening, empathy, and presence.

Afterward, I returned home shaken and in disbelief. My sense of well-being grew unsteady. Questions filled my mind while sleep eluded me, and I replayed the narratives over in my mind. My heart throbbed for them, and once more, I felt overcome with helplessness. As I lay waiting for sleep to come, I remembered another incident of violence when the crucifixion rocked the followers of Jesus. The confused and doubting disciples hid behind closed doors for fear of Jewish leaders. The future appeared full of unknowns, anxiety, and fright. They didn't understand Jesus would rise from the dead on the third day or comprehend the power of the resurrection.

While the disciples remained hidden, Jesus entered the locked room and said, "Peace be with you."

That restless night, I whispered Jesus' words, "Peace be with you." A calm came over me, and I let the Savior enter my anxiety. That moment transformed into a sacred moment of Christ's presence. I fell asleep.

---

*"The reality is that you will grieve forever.
You will not 'get over' the loss of a loved one; you will learn
to live with it. You will heal and you will rebuild
yourself around the loss you have suffered."*

—Elisabeth Kubler-Ross

Dear Jesus,

I lift my fears and anxieties to you. I lift those I love who also have fear. Come into my place of fear, bring peace. May I experience your companionship and closeness. Amen.

Reflect: When has a tragedy or disaster affected you?

Respond: How would Jesus respond to a tragedy?

Read: John 20

Journal Prompt: How did you respond to the tragedy or disaster?

Part 6

In the Presence of Mercy

Day 33

Come, Receive Mercy

*"Come to me, all you who are weary and burdened,
and I will give you rest."*

—Matthew 11:28

THOUGHT FOR THE DAY

Jesus invites us to come.

A PASTOR FRIEND played the song "Come as You Are" by David Crowder as the opening tune to a Service of Remembrance and Hope, encouraging all in attendance to bring their sadness. Each year, we offer a service for those who have lost loved ones, providing a safe place to grieve during the holiday season. The song set the mood for the service.

Crowder wrote the song to be invitational. When interviewed about the song, he said, "When we feel underserving, grace permits us to turn around and return home." All can approach God to find grace and relieve their burdens, hurts, and shame. How often do we get hit with thoughts of unworthiness because we can't control our grief? How frequently do we experience regret and brokenness when we mourn? The song beckons us to draw near to receive mercy.

Many express that grief leads to self-doubt, a sense of inadequacy, and fragility. Additionally, our emotions can fluctuate rapidly, leading to emotional distress within a short period. Coping with all these feelings can lead to fatigue. Indeed, one of the symptoms of grief is physical tiredness, which weighs us down. We wonder why we are more tired than usual and don't seem to see a reprieve. Crowder's song beckons us to come home to a compassionate God who understands our weaknesses.

Likewise, Jesus summons us with an open invitation to enter his presence and sit with him. The offer is available at any time without restrictions or qualifiers. Jesus invites us, "Come to me, all you who are weary and burdened, and I will give you rest." He offers rest for our heavy hearts by giving comfort and peace.

When we bring our burdens to Jesus, we can learn of his divine compassion, grace, and mercy. We will find rest for our weary souls, replacing the heaviness with peace. He takes all our regrets, fears, and inadequacies. Peace replaces the chaos of our emotions.

Our Savior invites us to draw near. Walking with Jesus in partnership means we are not alone in our grief. We don't need to handle life alone. The Son of God is willing to bear our woes and heavy burdens, making our load lighter and giving us a serenity that surpasses explanation.

"Come to Him in every and all circumstances.
He will not turn you away."

—Don MacLafferty

Dear welcoming Jesus,

I appear just as I am, not together, imperfect, and fragile. I bring my heavy burden of grief with my tiredness. Carry my burden, and give me peace and rest. Thank you for your free invitation. Amen.

Reflect: Reflect on the lyrics from "Come as You Are" by David Crowder or "Just as I Am" by Charlotte Elliot.

Respond: Accept Jesus' invitation to come.

Read: Hebrews 4:14–16

Journal Prompt: Write an invitation from God to come, using your name.

Day 34

Feel the Emotions

"Now my soul is troubled, and what shall I say?
'Father, save me from this hour'? No, it was for this very reason
I came to this hour. Father, glorify your name!"

—John 12:27–28

THOUGHT FOR THE DAY

Jesus experienced emotions.

WHEN C. S. Lewis lost his dear wife, Joy, he turned to writing to process his grief. Her death brought intense, raw emotions that engulfed him in such a way that frightened him. In his book *A Grief Observed*, he wrote, "No one ever told me that grief felt so like fear."[6] Later in a following passage, he wrote: "Feelings, and feelings, and feelings. Let me try thinking instead."[7] As a British literary scholar, writer, and intellectual giant, he wrote of midnight agonies, smashed dreams, miseries, impatience with others who said trite things, and bitterness. "You can't see anything properly while your eyes are blurred with tears." He writes of doubts about God's goodness after Joy, death."[8]

---

[6] C. S. Lewis, *A Grief Observed* (New York: Seabury Press, 1961), 7.
[7] Lewis, *A Grief Observed*, 31.
[8] Lewis, *A Grief Observed*, 37.

Contrary to the popular belief that burying emotions signifies strength, Lewis didn't hide his grief. He confronted it directly, feeling every emotion fully. Grief resembles a tunnel—you move through it to reach the other side, where healing begins. Studies have found that suppressing feelings creates strain on both mental and physical health.

Specifically, Jesus gives us a powerful example of acknowledging his feelings when he lived on Earth. Being fully divine and human, he experienced emotions and disclosed them. His display of vulnerability stood in stark contrast to stoicism. Christ showed compassion, distress, sadness, and weariness. As a man, he openly expressed what he felt without hesitation or shame when he wept over Jerusalem and wept at the death of Lazarus. When he observed the hurting crowd, he felt compassion for them in his ministry.

Hours before Jesus went to the cross, he prayed, "Now my soul is troubled, and what shall I say? 'Father, save me from this hour?'" Despite his inner turmoil and distress, our Savior obeyed the Father. Through prayer and tears, Christ showed his suffering and articulated his emotions.

Not only can we learn from Jesus, but we can also learn from Lewis, who used writing to express his emotions. Therefore, when sorrow seems unbearable and painful, lean into it, not away. God understands the struggle and the ways we process our feelings. Once we sit with the grief, we open ourselves to comfort and healing and thus begin moving forward. Acknowledge your emotions, sit with them, and invite Jesus into the midst of your grief.

"Ultimately, however, if you deny the emotions of your heart, you deny the essence of your life."

—Alan D. Wolfelt

Compassionate God,

I find it difficult to say what I am feeling. Please help me be okay with sitting with uncomfortable emotions. I invite you into my grief. Amen.

Reflect: What mode of communication do you use to acknowledge your emotions, such as writing, verbalizing, singing, tears, or prayer?

Respond: Use one mode of communication to admit your emotions.

Read: John 11:1–44

Journal Prompt: Explain why being honest about your feelings may be risky.

Day 35

He First Loved Us

"We love because he first loved us."

1 John 4:19

> ### THOUGHT FOR THE DAY
>
> Jesus suffers with us.

BEKAH BECAME MY friend after I learned her story of how God gave her grace and joy in the middle of extreme heartbreak when her son, Titus, was three years old. He was diagnosed with Batten disease, a rare degenerative condition.

The months that followed the diagnosis were months of writhing at the injustice of this horrid disease that gradually sucked the life out of her precious five-year-old. His care took every waking minute of her time as he deteriorated with constant seizures, oxygen dependence, inconsolable pain, and frequent 911 calls.

Even though she trusted that little Titus was on loan from God, it didn't take her anguish away. "How long does he have to suffer, Lord?" and then, with the same breath, she would pray, "Please don't let him die."[9]

---

[9] Bekah Bowman, *Can't Steal My Joy: The Journey to a Different Kind of Brave* (www.cantstealmyjoy: Kuna, Idaho, 2019), 137.

Bekah survived each day letting God know her emotions, telling God, she was struggling, felt cheated, damaged, beyond repair, totally shattered and broken. In her rage, she screamed at God, "What is happening? And where are you?" The standard niceties when something bad happens, such as "God works all things for good," turned her stomach.

When she was helpless to take away Titus's pain, she curled up in a ball, tears moistening the floor. An image came to her of a man hanging up on a cross, breathing labored, head drooped, and skin gaping open from being beaten. Nails were driven through his limbs, and blood was everywhere. At that moment, the man on the cross met her. He didn't give her answers or a promise to make everything better, but he identified with the brokenness her child was facing. There, hanging on the cross, Jesus reassured her, *"I know, daughter. I am here too."* Bekah knew Jesus was in the middle of all of her suffering. The image of Jesus' love carried her through the remaining months of Titus's life.

A seedling grew from an overturned pot on Bekah's porch into a bright yellow flower, Titus's favorite color. The stem later became damaged, but the bloom remained glorious and strong due to the roots. Later, Bekah wrote a book, *Can't Steal My Joy*, using a sketch of a potted yellow bloom with a bent stem. She wrote, "Our hope is not based on life storms that come at us, but in a consistent prom-ise-keeping God."[10] We exist beyond our fragile stems, living instead deep in our roots. Bekah is a living testament to God's grace: "We love because he first loved us."

Allow your roots to go deep in Christ and draw strength from the roots.

"No matter how long it's been, there are times when it suddenly becomes harder to breathe."

—Anonymous

---

[10] Bowman, *Can't Steal My Joy*, 173.

Lord Jesus,

I am broken and need your mercy and grace. Hold me, comfort me in this time of suffering. In Jesus' name, amen.

Reflect: When did you feel a sense of injustice?

Respond: Dwell on how much Christ loves you.

Read: 1 John 4:4–20

Journal Prompt: Write about that sense of injustice and how you found peace.

Day 36

God Hears

"Hear my cry for mercy as I call to you for help,
as I lift up my hands toward your Most Holy Place."

—Psalm 28:2

ZANE COULD NO longer continue working at the traffic center. His supervisors failed to support him, leaving him stuck at an impasse. Since high school, he dreamed of becoming an air traffic controller, dedicating himself to college aviation studies, working at airports, undergoing intensive FAA training, and moving to begin an apprenticeship. He said, "I lost more than a job; I lost a sense of purpose more than anything. I felt like the rug was pulled out from under me."

After leaving, depression seeped in like early morning fog and left him paralyzed. He'd spent nine years preparing for this, only to watch the dream vanish.

Zane's career disappointment isn't unique to him. Likewise, God gave Moses a job to free the Israelites from Egypt. Pharaoh's heart was hardened, causing Moses to accuse God: "Why, Lord, why have you brought trouble on this people? Is this why you sent me?"

(Exodus 5:22). Moses' words contained a lament, a passionate expression of deep distress and grief, and a complaint.

A lament humbly turns to God with our honest and unfiltered emotions, albeit doubt, anger, displeasure, disillusionment, or blame. It takes faith to lay our pain and questions before the Lord. A prayer of lament is not a polite church prayer but rather an honest expression of how we feel.

In fact, the book of Psalms includes sixty-five such prayers. The entire book of Lamentations is a conversation with the prophet Jeremiah, who expressed intense sorrow, questions, and confusion. From these laments, we learn it is okay to articulate our gut-wrenching feelings to the Almighty and then to appeal for mercy.

When we express our grievances to God, it shows that we believe enough to challenge God. Just saying the words stir up trust in the Faithful One, even though we don't understand: "Hear my cry for mercy as I call to you for help." Once we ask for mercy, a turning occurs, sometimes repentance, but always trust. Then in faith we thank God: "Praise be to the LORD, for he has heard my cry for mercy" (Psalm 28:6).

We have permission to bemoan and ask why we lost a job or why a loved one died. If godly individuals in the Bible lamented, then we can too. God heard their complaint. In addition, lament plays a vital role in deepening our relationship with the Holy One. It serves as a prayer that bridges the gap between what has occurred and what we trust will come to pass.

"Lamenting is the spiritual mature response to sadness and sorrow. Our spiritual aliveness is not found in our ability to suppress our sadness."

—Rich Villodas

Merciful God,

I pour out my complaint like water. My loss overwhelms me. You know the pain because Christ also suffered grief. Listen to my prayers, and thank you for your faithfulness. Amen.

Reflect: How did you feel when you lost a job or a career?

Respond: It's okay to complain or be angry.

Read: Lamentations 3:19–33

Journal Prompt: Write a lament to God about your loss—no need to be polite.

Unfailing Love

"I have loved you with an everlasting love;
I have drawn you with unfailing kindness."

—Jeremiah 31:3

THOUGHT FOR THE DAY

God loves you unconditionally.

"NICOLE, HOW ARE you doing? I missed you," I said after she missed several business meetings.

Her answer caught me off guard when she answered, "Not good. I lost my grandmother." Tears welled in her eyes, and her voice quivered as she said, "She was like a mother to me. I lived with her when I was a teenager . . . She took me to church."

Then Nicole retold the last few weeks of her ninety-six-year-old grandma's life. "I was with her when she died."

"I am so glad you were with her. I'm sure it was comforting to her for you to be with her." The final moments of life are sacred as the boundary between heaven and earth grows thin, and we often experience a profound sense of the Holy One's presence.

Nicole felt blessed with a kind and supportive grandmother who played a vital role in nurturing her faith. Many grandparents share wisdom, offer encouragement, give unreserved love, celebrate their successes and devote undistracted time.

When we lose a grandparent or someone who is supportive and kind like a grandparent, we lament because we lost the person who loved us in an irreplaceable way. We lose how they cherished us. We also mourn the lost security and the legacy of the past. Equally, their love transcended our circumstances, and they surrounded us with favor. Taking comfort in their memories helps but the hole is still there.

Most importantly, God's love is nurturing, absolute, and limitless, like that of a grandparent who gives generously, is always present, and offers hugs regardless of our deeds. Scripture reminds us of the Lord's love: "I have loved you with an everlasting love; I have drawn you with unfailing kindness." Other Scriptures echo this truth. For example, Psalm 36:7 declares, "How priceless is your unfailing love, O God!" and 1 Chronicles 16:34 reminds us, "His love endures forever." The Most Holy God deeply cherishes us. Indeed, God's devotion to us remains constant and unwavering regardless of our actions or words. If we need forgiveness, he is faithful in forgiving when asked. Despite our messing up, he offers us wholehearted love and safety in his arms. Nothing we could ever do will change the Faithful One's unfailing love for us.

"God's love for you is unconditional and undeserved."

—Cru

Dear loving God,

May you embrace me with your everlasting and unconditional love, walk before me to guide me, be beside me to give me courage, be beneath me for support, and be behind me to keep me safe. Amen.

Reflect: In what ways do you experience God's unlimited love?

Respond: Express thankfulness for the good memories you have.

Read: Romans 8:26–39

Journal Prompt: Share a time when you felt loved unconditionally.

(Check out in the back of the book, How to Have a Relationship with Jesus).

Day 38

Nearness of God

"The LORD is near to all who call on him,
to all who call on him in truth."

—Psalm 145:18

THOUGHT FOR THE DAY

The Lord is unwavering in his presence.

"WHERE DID THIS come from?" Susan told a friend when a memory ignited sorrow, loneliness, and regret. The resurfaced emotions caught her by surprise because she thought she had moved through the most intense part of grieving.

Valentine's Day always held a special meaning when her husband was alive. Now, the day took on a different meaning, melancholy and remembering what once was.

She is not the only one who gets triggered by holidays. Likewise, for many, birthdays, anniversaries, and holidays trigger emotions like a tsunami wave, knocking us off our feet and taking our breath away. Embedded in special occasions are traditions that bring up memories of a loved one lost or of another kind of loss, such as a divorce, a lost friendship, or a move. Memories spark reminders of whom or what we have lost, leading to sadness. We yearn for what we lost, wishing it would be different and we dream of one more time.

When sorrow overpowers us, we can lose sight of God's presence. Regardless of how we feel, the Sovereign God remains with us and understands our pain, as we see in Psalm 38:9: "All my longings lie open before you, Lord; my sighing is not hidden from you." Even when our trust wavers or fear consumes us, the Lord is unwavering in his presence.

A faithful man in the Old Testament named Daniel experienced anguish and weakness when he saw a vision that alarmed and frightened him to the point of being unable to breathe. An angel said to him, "Don't be afraid . . . Peace! Be encouraged! Be strong!" (Daniel 10:19 NLT). God's words enabled Daniel to trust God's plan.

Although we may not receive a vision or be visited by an angel when the reality of our loss hits us, we can be confident that the Almighty hears our prayers. In the same way, as the Almighty uplifted and supported Daniel, he promises to be near when we call on him. "The LORD is near to all who call on him, to all who call on him in truth."

Spiritual strength and inner resources will come when needed. God sent neighbors to Susan this year with flowers and chocolates for Valentine's Day. God came near through her neighbors. God will come through for you.

"What we have once enjoyed deeply we can never lose. All that we love deeply becomes a part of us."

—Helen Keller

Dear ever-present God,

Thank you for your promise to be close when I call on you. Wrap me in your arms, and comfort me when sadness knocks me down. Amen.

Reflect: Imagine yourself wrapped in the Lord's arms.

Respond: When overwhelmed with sad memories, pray to experience God's closeness.

Read: Psalm 73

Journal Prompt: What triggers emotions from your loss during special occasions? Write down ideas that will help you through.

Day 39

God Is Trustworthy

"It's impossible to please God apart from faith. And why? Because anyone who wants to approach God must believe both that he exists and that he cares enough to respond to those who seek him."

—Hebrews 11:6 MSG

THOUGHT FOR THE DAY

We can trust the character of God.

LAURA STORY, A renowned Christian artist and worship leader, has experienced deep heartache. During a singing tour, she miscarried. She recalls the deep sadness of that moment and how she continued performing her planned concert, knowing nothing could change the outcome. One of the songs she sang, "God of Every Story," reminded her to hold on to the truth of God's faithfulness.

When the miscarriage occurred, shock muddled her mind, and sorrow flooded in. She grieved the loss of a loved baby who would never experience life outside the womb or feel her embrace. Laura tried to tough it out but began questioning God's ways. She wrestled and finally recognized that some losses in life defy understanding. As a result, Laura put her trust in a faithful God for what she couldn't see and trusted God through the heartache.

In her book *I Give Up,* Laura writes, "We are called to believe God in the messy middle of our story when sorrow and grief threaten to railroad belief. We are called to believe God for the long view, for the ending we can't yet see."[11]

Like Laura most losses bring unanswered questions. We cognitively know God is love and wants the best for us. However, our emotions deceive us, causing us to feel that a mistake has occurred. Beyond what we feel, we can ask God to comfort us, take what we experience, and use it.

Indeed, we are not alone. The Old Testament tells stories of saints who trusted God despite not receiving the answers to their prayers. Their circumstances proved untidy and difficult. Hebrews 11 highlights the unwavering faith of these saints who focused on the future despite not understanding the present. They trusted confidently, even without seeing what lay ahead.

Laura was no stranger to sorrow before her miscarriage. A few years before the pregnancy loss, her husband underwent surgery for a brain tumor, leaving him disabled, probably for life. During that time, she sang about God seeing each tear fall and embracing us in the palm of his hand.

When we face unexpected loss, our hope rests in the character of a faithful, trustworthy God who continues to shape our path and uses those difficult losses in our lives and the lives of others. Most assuredly, we can trust God to write our story.

"When God makes promises, he is trustworthy to keep those promises. He will keep them without fail."

—Karen Hoffman

---

[11] Laura Story, *I Give Up: The Secret Joy of a Surrendered Life* (Thomas Nelson, 2019), 129.

Trustworthy God,

Enable me to trust you in the messy middle of loss when I don't have answers. May I look to you instead of my circumstances. Steady me. Amen.

Reflect: Think about how God is trustworthy.

Respond: Turn your gaze to God, rather than your situation.

Read: Hebrews 11

Journal Prompt: The saints in Hebrews 11 often didn't receive the promise of faith. Write about a question you have concerning your loss.

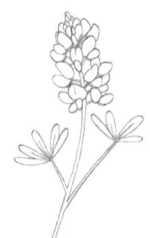

Part 7

Encounters with Grace

Day 40

God Doesn't Waste Our Pain

"You intended to harm me, but God intended it for good."

—Genesis 50:20

"AM I A good person?" my brother, David, questioned after his divorce. The entire world seemed broken, and questions of self-doubt haunted him. On a personal level, he contended with betrayal, rejection, anger, and intense disappointment. "More than the loss of my wife was the loss of my sense of family because I grew up with a strong sense of family. It had a long-term effect on me," he said. "Putting the kids on a plane every other Christmas was the hardest part."

David suffered multiple losses. His family view had to adjust so that he could move forward. With loss comes a change to the new reality; he was now a single dad raising two little girls. Life would never be the same.

In my experience, grief becomes who we are, and we won't ever recover from it entirely, but we can be reconciled to it. We reshape our worldview in response to what has occurred, whether it is a divorce or another kind of loss. It takes time for the torn heart to mend and for resolution to occur.

We see this in the Old Testament's example of Joseph, who faced immense trials and hardship when his brothers sold him into slavery, separating him from his family, culture, language, and everything he knew. Taken to a foreign land, he served as a servant in Potiphar's house, only to be betrayed by Potiphar's wife. This deception led Joseph to unjust imprisonment for twelve years (Genesis 37–45).

Despite these hardships, Joseph consistently found favor in all he did, acknowledging the Lord. We are not given details, but Joseph reached a point where he reconciled his grief, humbled himself before the Lord, and chose forgiveness. In time, God elevated Joseph, granting him the wisdom and favor to manage Egypt during a severe famine. When his brothers from Canaan came seeking help, Joseph saved them, fulfilling God's redemption plan. Joseph answered his brothers, "You intended to harm me, but God intended it for good" (Genesis 50:20).

When I asked David what helped him through those tough days, he replied, "Somehow I wanted God to use this to help someone else." His response reflected a deep faith and hope that his pain could serve a greater purpose.

As God ultimately used Joseph's suffering to save many lives, our pain is never wasted in God's hands. Through our trials, God often works to deepen our reliance on him, shape our character, and use us to help others. God can bring redemption and purpose.

*"Your pain is the key that opens your heart
and ushers you on your healing."*

—Alan D. Wolfelt

Dear Lord,

Please give me the grace to adjust and reconcile my grief. Transform my pain into something you can use. Amen.

Reflect: How has God used your pain?

Respond: Ask God to help you come to terms with your loss.

Read: Genesis 37 and 39

Journal Prompt: Describe how God has shaped your character through your loss.

All-Surpassing Power of God

*"But we have this treasure in jars of clay to show that this
all-surpassing power is from God and not from us."*

—2 Corinthians 4:7

THOUGHT FOR THE DAY

The Holy Spirit lives inside us to renew us.

I STOOD AT my dad's bedside in the hospital, holding his hand
and reassuring him that Jesus had prepared a place for him. Within
minutes, he took his last breath, a peaceful expression settling on
his face. At that moment, my breath caught, and his absence frightened me. *How could I go on? Dad always stood by me.* Panic filled
me, and the finality of his death struck like a thunderclap. My hero,
constant cheerleader, and protector, especially when I was a single
mother, had died. Now I was fatherless, and I struggled to breathe.

Although he suffered from a prolonged illness, I was not ready
to let him go. Dread gripped me at the idea of facing life without
him. Shock set in, making driving difficult and clouding my ability
to focus on work. The heartache led to a loss of motivation, draining
me of energy. I felt fragile, much like a breakable pot.

The Bible calls us clay jars, brittle earthenware. While we are
vulnerable, God has placed in us a treasure: the presence of the

Holy Spirit. "But we have this treasure in jars of clay to show that this all-surpassing power is from God and not from us." When we receive Christ, the Holy Spirit comes into our human spirit; as a result, the power of God resides in us. The Holy Spirit strengthens us and enables us to make it through mourning. Outwardly, we may be breakable, but within, the surpassing strength of God is ours.

God's presence keeps us from being crushed when we experience grief. Our minds may waver, and our emotions crumble from the impact of sorrow, but we need not despair, for the eternal God gives us what we lack. In fact, "Inwardly we are being renewed day by day" (2 Corinthians 4:16). The unparalleled power of God renews us and provides us with inner strength. I witnessed the inner strength during that time after I lost my father. God enabled me to get through.

We often ask, "When will I be healed of this grief?" Healing will not occur until we are in Jesus's presence. Therefore, we can set our gaze on the unseen because the seen is temporary, but the unseen is eternal.

"When we think of life in terms of things being impermanent it has the ability to shift our perceptions."

—Carly Benson

All-powerful and eternal God,

Be my support. Renew me. I am weak; be my courage. Please help me to focus on your promises and see what is everlasting. In Jesus' name, amen.

Reflect: How has God given you strength in your loss when you were weak?

Respond: If you are unsure of knowing Jesus, acknowledge your need for him and ask him to be in your life. A guide on how to know Jesus is in the back of the book.

Read: 2 Corinthians 4:7–18

Journal Prompt: Describe how you let the Holy Spirit renew you when you seemed the lowest.

Sustaining Grace

*"Cast your cares on the Lᴏʀᴅ and he will sustain you;
he will never let the righteous be shaken."*

—Psalm 55:22

<u>**Tʜᴏᴜɢʜᴛ ꜰᴏʀ ᴛʜᴇ Dᴀʏ**</u>

God will sustain you.

RAQUEL EXPERIENCED ISOLATION after her husband's death from cancer. Dark voices of despair whispered, *What's the point?* Physical and emotional exhaustion gripped her as gloom churned through her mind, filling her with fear. "Holding all these things inside me felt so hard," Raquel said. "And I had no way to let them out."

During this time, Raquel prayed but wondered if God listened. Over the next year, she joined the grief group I led, met with a counselor, and became part of a widows' group. She discovered that her emotions reflected a regular part of the grieving process. Connecting with other widows who understood her journey brought immense relief. All these avenues offered a safe place to share her ups and downs and connect with others. A friend encouraged her to get more involved in church and Bible study. After getting involved, she was able to say, "Grief was not debilitating anymore."

Psalm 55 provides a powerful prayer in which the writer expresses his distress. God seemed distant during the psalmist's trials, but David continued to call for aid. He openly described his mental anguish and his pounding heart. David yearned to escape his difficulties, wishing for flight like a bird—much like Raquel's experience with her isolation. Nevertheless, he prayed, "Evening, morning and noon I cry out in distress, and he hears my voice" (Psalm 55:17).

After David expressed his pain to the Lord, he found renewed assurance that the Holy One would care for his concerns. He declared, "Cast your cares on the LORD and he will sustain you; he will never let the righteous be shaken. . . . But as for me, I trust in you" (Psalm 55:22–23).

Similarly, for Raquel, through those intense times of sadness and depletion, God provided her with others to walk beside her: a grief group, a counselor, a widows' group, and a Bible study group. God sustained her. Over time, her grief gave way to healing.

When experiencing distress, call out to God and look for ways to connect with others. Connecting with others helps us know we are not alone and hastens healing. The grace of a loving God will come to your aid and sustain you. In time, the darkness will give way to light.

"Sustaining grace promises not the absence of struggle but the presence of God."

—Max Lucado

Dear Holy One,

When I am weary in the morning, strengthen me.
When I am tired at noon, revive me.
When I am depleted in the evening, refresh me.
When the trial devastates me, transcend my circumstances.
When grief seems too big, hold me and refuel my emotions.
When stress is overwhelming, sustain me with your grace.
Holy One, refresh me as the rain refreshes the dry earth. Amen.

Reflect: Meditate on David's prayer in Psalm 55.

Respond: Reach out to a group with a similar loss.

Read: Psalm 55

Journal Prompt: Describe one emotion you felt this week from your loss.

God Carries Our Anxieties

"Cast all your anxiety on him because he cares for you."

—1 Peter 5:7

THOUGHT FOR THE DAY

God cares about every concern.

MY FATHER USED his well-worn wheelbarrow for many manual tasks. I can still picture him in the yard loading rocks, dirt, or sod into this piece of equipment and dumping the contents in another place. He valued how it minimized his workload by carrying heavy objects or messy things like cement, and it was probably his favorite tool. In fact, one of the first tools Dad gave my husband was a secondhand wheelbarrow.

Likewise, I often think of how I accumulate anxieties like rocks I carry around, placing them one by one in my wheelbarrow. At first, I can push that device, but when I add more and more rocks, I make the wheelbarrow too heavy to move. With all my concerns piled high, my wheelbarrow won't budge, and I must discard some of the stones.

Anxieties come in all forms, but after a loss, we experience grief and other vulnerable emotions, such as fear of the future, confusion about why this happened, worry about finances, and even anger. A widow frets about how to take care of her bills after her spouse dies. A recently divorced man worries about seeing his kids. After multiple miscarriages, a woman agonizes over her losses and wonders if she will ever be able to carry a child to full term. Panic comes when someone fears a holiday without their loved one. These anxieties seem too much to bear. How much can we endure? Our wheelbarrow is overflowing.

Thankfully, we don't have to carry the load by ourselves. In 1 Peter 5:7, Peter instructs us to cast all our cares and worries on the Lord. Because our Heavenly Father cares for us, he invites us to give all our worries to him. We don't have to lift them ourselves but can cast them away. In that verse, the Greek word for cast means to throw as one would throw a baseball once and for all.

As with my illustration, we can intentionally dump our wheelbarrow of worries at the foot of the Lord and leave them there. We can take all worries, big or small, to God. A compassionate and loving God listens, empathizes, and knows our needs. We can throw each anxiety on the Lord, who will carry it.

"Anxiety is a signal alerting you that it's time to pray."

—Craig Groeschel

Dear Heavenly Father, who cares for me,

I carry many heavy loads of anxiety, fears, and emotions that weigh me down and distract me from joy and peace. Please help me hand over my concerns and leave them with you. May your peace strengthen me, your grace sustains me, and your presence bring me consolation. Thank you for being a God who loves and cares. Amen.

Reflect: Picture yourself dumping your worries at the foot of the Lord.

Respond: Note the times of day or experiences that lead to anxiety.

Read: Matthew 6:25–34

Journal Prompt: Name your specific concerns and create a prayer giving them to God.

Day 44

Lost Dreams and Hopes

*"I have told you these things, so that in me you may have peace.
In this world you will have trouble. But take heart!
I have overcome the world."*

—John 16:33

> ### THOUGHT FOR THE DAY
>
> Jesus overcomes the trials of this world.

MARIA WORKED HARD cleaning houses and studying English to become a naturalized U.S. citizen. She and her husband raised four children in a close-knit family, giving them love, support, and an excellent education. Her oldest daughter had a child out of wedlock and didn't want to care for the baby, leaving him for Maria to raise. After that, her daughter moved in with a female partner. Maria cried and cried, talked to her priest, and finally saw a counselor, trying to reconcile what happened to her daughter.

Some of us struggle with our children's choices, often defying our expectations. They might be in relationships we disapprove of, struggling with addiction, living on the fringes of society, estranged from us, involved in illegal activities that lead to incarceration, or making other choices that weigh heavily on our hearts. Regardless of their decisions, shattered dreams remain, like a vase crashing to the floor, breaking into hundreds of pieces. We grieve over their lives and the potential losses that are fracturing our hopes for them. With grief emerges all the emotions associated with it—sadness, anger, hurt, fear, self-doubt, and guilt.

Our grief is not unlike that of the apostle Paul, who started a church in the city of Corinth. Shortly after he left, he regretfully learned of sexual immorality, divisions, and disregard for his teaching. Paul mourned over the situation and their behavior. "For I wrote you out of great distress and anguish of heart and with many tears, not to grieve you but to let you know the depth of my love for you" (2 Corinthians 2:4).

While on Earth, we live in a fallen world where illness, personal choices, sin, and the actions of others shape our experiences. We are deeply affected and encounter immense pain, sorrow, and numerous hardships. Jesus Christ suffered for this broken world by going to the cross to atone for humanity's sins, thus providing a way of salvation for those who trust in him.

Christ doesn't exempt us from pain, but instead we can join in the sufferings of Christ. We align our hardships and trials with the suffering the Savior endured on the cross. My friend Michael brings this perspective: "In pain, we share in the suffering of Christ."

We receive a promise: "In this world you will have trouble. But take heart! I have overcome the world."

"Everyone suffers, even the good Lord suffered when he was on Earth."

—Wilson Rawls

Father God,

I long for all to be made right. Until then, comfort me and heal the pain I feel. May I experience your presence. Amen.

Reflect: Contemplate on the sufferings of Christ.

Respond: Pray and commit your lost dreams to God.

Read: Psalm 22:1–11

Journal Prompt: Write about a lost dream and what was lost.

Day 45

All-Knowing and All-Present God

"Before a word is on my tongue you, LORD,
know it completely. You hem me in behind and before,
and you lay your hand upon me."

—Psalm 139:4–5

HAVE YOU EVER experienced abandonment after losing a loved one or another kind of loss?

Ryan grew up in a parsonage with his parents while his father pastored the church. At three years old, he watched his mother battle a devastating illness. Despite her strength and determination to fight, she lost her battle when Ryan turned seven.

"She died in the hospital, and I never got the chance to say goodbye to the person who was the bedrock of my young life," he recalled. "Even though she fought to stay with us, I couldn't shake the feeling of abandonment." To add to this, he experienced loneliness, vulnerability, and fright without his mother, and as a child, he was unable to express those feelings.

However, the church community surrounded Ryan and his siblings with tenderness, love, and care. Every day after school, he stopped by the church office, where Beth, the secretary, welcomed him. She became a surrogate mother to him, listening to his stories, asking about his day, and making sure someone cared for him and his siblings until his father finished work. God lovingly provided for this young boy. As the eldest of three, Ryan carried a heavy sense of responsibility beyond his years, making his childhood far from typical.

Just as God recognized and understood Ryan's needs, God also comprehends us even before we verbalize our own needs. "Before a word is on my tongue, you, LORD, know it completely. You hem me in behind and before, and you lay your hand upon me." The Creator of heaven and earth will encircle us with love, protection, and support. An all-knowing God understands our sorrows, losses, hurts, regrets, fears, doubts, and longings. The psalmist tells us that God sees us no matter what: "Where can I go from your Spirit? Where can I flee from your presence?" (Psalm 139:7). God knows and understands.

Today, Ryan is transforming his childhood pain into a source of compassion by helping others. He volunteers as a leader in his church and shares his story with groups. Because of what he experienced as a child, he helps children in Malawi by raising funds to buy dolls for those who may have no other toys. Ryan turned his unwanted grief into something impactful and purposeful. Allow God to turn your unwanted loss into a way to help others.

"There is no grief like the grief that does not speak."

—Henry Wordsworth

All-knowing and ever-present God,

You know my feelings entirely, and even in your vastness, you never forget me. "How precious to me are your thoughts, God! How vast is the sum of them! Were I to count them, they would outnumber the grains of sand—when I awake, I am still with you" (Psalm 139:17–18). Amen.

Reflect: Envision God entering your life during this time of grief.

Respond: Allow the Holy Spirit to console you in your grief.

Read: Psalm 139

Journal Prompt: Write a note of gratitude to God for seeing and knowing you right where you are now.

God Forgives

"Godly sorrow brings repentance that leads to salvation and leaves no regret, but worldly sorrow brings death."

—2 Corinthians 7:10

> ### THOUGHT FOR THE DAY
>
> Grace gives a second chance.

AS A CHAPLAIN, I visited Sean McIntyre, a freckle-faced, red-haired man in his thirties dressed in shorts and a T-shirt, which was not the typical attire for the hospital. Tension and melancholy lingered in his green eyes, reflecting the weight of his struggles. He committed himself to detoxification, and I noticed the trembling in his body from withdrawal. I wondered if his body mirrored the turmoil within. With raw honesty, he admitted, "Drank too much, too often. The drinking has affected my health and my family," his voice laced with defeat and brokenness.

His confession revealed the painful truth—his self-destructive behavior had cost him his wife and young child. Remorse filled his words as he confessed. Yet in his sorrow, he also showed resolution. "I don't want to lose my family. I want to be a good dad to my three-year-old son."

Regret simultaneously intertwined with grief became his wake-up call. The consequence of his choices propelled him toward change, forcing him to confront the giant of addiction and commit himself. He found the courage to reclaim what mattered most in the searing pain of loss, his family. He cried, with an intense desire to change.

To rephrase, regret is a deep sadness, grief, repentance, or disappointment over past actions or missed opportunities. Overcoming remorse takes courage, as Mr. McIntyre did when he committed to recovery. He confessed his wrong to me. Scripture assures us, "Godly sorrow brings repentance that leads to salvation and leaves no regret."

Then he acknowledged his need for mercy. I let him know that God promises to forgive: "If we confess our sins, he is faithful and will forgive us our sins and purify us from all unrighteousness" (1 John 1:9). He nodded his head when I asked him about including God in his recovery. We prayed for God to help him become sober, change his behavior and life, and give him fortitude.

My patient in the hospital showed me that regret is a kind of loss. Indeed, God delights in giving us a second chance, a reflection of divine grace. That is why Christ came to give us a fresh start and empower us to follow him. If regret is part of your loss, ask for forgiveness, resolve to change, and ask God to strengthen you to take the next step.

"God's grace is bigger than your biggest regret."

—Lecrae

Forgiving God,

I have messed up my life. You know the grief I feel for my decisions. Please forgive me and give me strength and courage to follow you. Thank you for your forgiveness. In Jesus' name, amen.

Reflect: Examine ways your past mistakes can lead to change and growth.

Respond: Reorient your soul to a good and forgiving God. Ask for forgiveness if needed.

Read: Psalm 51

Journal Prompt: Write a prayer asking God to give you what you need.

Part 8

When Hope Breaks Through

Day 47

New Mercies

"Great is his faithfulness;
his mercies begin afresh each morning."

—Lamentations 3:23 NLT

THOUGHT FOR THE DAY

God greets us daily with new mercies.

THE BEAUTIFUL PIANO music filled my living room, and the melodious tune swept me away with emotion. Mae, a gifted pianist, often plays for us at our home Bible study. My eighty-one-year-old neighbor has spent a lifetime playing for churches and teaching music. Recently, she shared a prayer request after losing a dear friend from kindergarten. Mae comments, "Thank God for Zoom. I can attend the funeral by Zoom."

In addition, Mae lost six friends and a few cousins this year. She relies on watching the funerals online since she lives in another state from the close-knit community and church in Brooklyn, New York, where she grew up. Mae is no stranger to grief, a widow for almost twenty years. However, this season has been incredibly challenging, with multiple deaths.

When I visited her, I asked, "Mae, how do you manage with so many losses?" Her ebony face glows, revealing a few wrinkles.

"Family and friends, many of whom I have known since elementary school, are all lovers of Jesus," she says.

"Music is a great comfort to me. I sing and praise God." She illustrates this by humming a few lines from "I Come to the Garden Alone." Then she moves from the couch to her baby grand, and with expression and passion she plays "I Surrender All." I sing the words, and my eyes fill with tears.

She switches from talking about herself to speaking to me: "Surrendering to God is difficult but powerful." She compares a daily gym workout to a daily surrender, explaining that we get stronger the more we do it.

Then she returns to the sofa. "Life is for a season. We never know when any of us will go." Using words from the old hymn "Great Is Thy Faithfulness," she sings, "Morning by morning, new mercies, I see." Mae continues, "I rely on new mercies each day to give me strength, his steadfast love and goodness."

Often, daily burdens overwhelm us before we have a moment to catch our breath. Nevertheless, embodying Mae, we can trust God's fresh mercies daily. We can rely on the goodness of the Lord to meet us anew each day.

"God is with us through Christ and, by the Spirit, his promises for new mercies are as real and trustworthy today as they were yesterday."

—Dave Zuleger

God of mercy,

This day seems overwhelming. Join me in all my brokenness, and send your blessings and love. Help me surrender to you. Amen.

Reflect: Ponder the words to a song that brings comfort.

Respond: Start your day with an expectation of new mercies.

Read: Psalm 62

Journal Prompt: Write a prayer of surrender.

Day 48

Help My Unbelief

"I do believe; help me overcome my unbelief!"

—Mark 9:24

THOUGHT FOR THE DAY

God gives mercy and faith when needed.

MY JOB AS a hospital chaplain involved helping individuals find comfort and encouragement in their faith. I often help them identify their emotions and help them connect with their faith. One patient stands out in my mind: Mr. Jose Fuentes. As I stepped into the room, Mr. Fuentes sat slumped in his hospital bed, his face etched with anguish. His dark eyes, glossy with unshed tears, met mine.

"They just told me," he started, in trembling speech, "they must amputate my leg to stop the infection."

"I don't want to lose it," he whispered, his voice thick with emotion. "But if I don't"—he swallowed hard—"the infection will kill me."

When he spoke again, his words came slowly with his Spanish accent. "I work in construction. I've done it my whole life. How . . . how will I provide for my family?"

"I am so sorry for your loss. You are losing not only your leg but also your way of making a living. Lots of losses and lots of grief," I said.

My heart overflowed with compassion for this man. Though unworthy and unsure how to comfort him, I turned to prayer. Then I began to share the story of two sisters, Mary and Martha, who came to Jesus in their sorrow. Their brother, Lazarus, had died, and they were consumed by grief. When Jesus saw their pain—the loss of his dear friend and the anguish of those left behind—he was deeply moved. In that moment of shared sorrow, Jesus wept with them.

"Our Savior understands your suffering and hurts with you," I said to Mr. Fuentes. He nodded as he fingered a Rosary. "The Savior suffered too."

After a pause, .

I spoke gently, "It's okay to be honest with God and tell him you're scared . . . It's okay to cry for your loss and not always be strong." His eyes met mine as I continued.

"Two prayers God hears are, *I do believe; help me overcome my unbelief.* And *God, have mercy,*" I said.

Tears soon welled in Mr. Fuentes's brown eyes and spilled down his cheeks. His shoulders shook as he surrendered to his grief. I reached out my hand and touched his shoulder. After waiting a while, I prayed with him and entrusted him to the Savior's care, praying that God would meet him in his tears.

Losing health is a huge loss that we have a right to grieve over and allow ourselves to take time to process. God's promises will lead us to strength beyond ourselves and to light for the journey. Weep if needed; Christ will meet you in your tears.

> *"Grief is like going through a tunnel—and sometimes we wonder if we'll ever come out the other end. But God has not abandoned you, and He wants to comfort you and assure you that He is with you. Jesus' words are true: 'Blessed are those who mourn, for they will be comforted' (Matthew 5:4)."*
>
> —Billy Graham

Good and forgiving God,

My pain and sadness defy description. I believe, but help my unbelief. Please be merciful to me. In Jesus' name, amen.

Reflect: Contemplate God's mercy and compassion.

Respond: Allow yourself to cry.

Read: Mark 5:21–43

Journal Prompt: Write about a time when you felt hopeless and what happened as a result.

Day 49

God Delights in You

"He will take great delight in you; in his love he will no longer rebuke you, but will rejoice over you with singing."

—Zephaniah 3:17

THOUGHT FOR THE DAY

God rejoices over you.

I AM THE queen of yellow sticky notes! Little golden reminders fill my house, helping me keep track of my to-dos and ensuring that nothing important slips my attention. But a significant reminder stands out—it concerns God's love for me. I attached the Zephaniah verse in a massive font to my bathroom mirror. "He will take great delight in you; in his love he will no longer rebuke you, but will rejoice over you with singing." It's my daily assurance that God takes pleasure in me, and the verse reminds me of his consistent love.

When we experience a loss, we flounder in grief while our emotions and thoughts waver, sometimes causing us to perceive we are unloved and unworthy. We question, *How could God love me? He took away someone special from me. Why did that loss happen? What is wrong with me?* Negative self-talk creeps in during times of grief and vulnerability, repeating itself in our minds over and over. Those thoughts make it challenging to comprehend that the

God of creation loves us and takes pleasure in us. Our loss doesn't define our worth; it is a sorrow we endure in a world marred by brokenness. No matter how inadequate we believe ourselves to be, God desires a connection with us. Counter negative thoughts with thoughts of God delighting in you. What a concept that the Lord savors hearing about our day and our concerns! The God of the universe celebrates over us with gladness.

The last part of the verse ends with telling us he "will rejoice over [us] with singing." When I am happy, I fill my spaces with melodies, whether in my house, on the patio, or in the car. How about you? The Lord's unconditional, grace-filled love rejoices over us with songs. May this truth of the Heavenly Father's tenderness seep into our pores. Our understanding of his fondness for us empowers us to live each day with confidence.

Conversely, grieving nonstop isn't healthy, as it strains both body and mind. Taking breaks to engage in pleasurable activities—such as painting, meeting a friend for coffee, playing golf, or attending a concert—helps restore balance and supports healing. Make time to take a break from grieving and do something pleasurable.

"Just like you have to give yourself permission to grieve, you need to give yourself permission to feel the emotion of happiness. ... Laughter is not going to take away the pain, but it will help you get through the pain."

—Sarah Philpott

Dear loving God,

You care for me more than my limited mind can understand, and you find pleasure in me. Let this truth penetrate the inner recesses of my heart so that I can start each day with assurance, knowing I am the object of your delight. Give me joy so that I may sing songs to you. Amen.

Reflect: Meditate on God's love for you.

Respond: Permit yourself to do something that brings pleasure.

Read: Psalm 118

Journal Prompt: Make a list of what gives you joy.

Day 50

Grief Changes Us

"I can do all this through him who gives me strength."

—Philippians 4:13

THOUGHT FOR THE DAY

Christ will give you the strength needed.

I MET JENNIFER after the sudden death of her husband. He fought leukemia for years, but every time it recurred, he bounced back. However, one time, he struggled to stay awake, and the doctor admitted him to the ICU. After a few days on the ventilator, the doctor said, "There is nothing we can do. Let him go."

Immediately, grief clouded Jennifer's thoughts, and sadness and desperation filled her heart. His passing struck Jennifer unexpectedly, leaving her unprepared and struggling to locate essential papers. As the shock diminished, anger rose in its place—anger at him for never revealing the extent of his illness. She grappled with a sense of betrayal. As the resentment subsided, she started noticing everything he did for her, things she once ignored. Later, regret emerged for not cherishing her spouse enough.

Meanwhile, she wrote in her journal, "I have to go on without him. . . . I am not the same person I was when Scott was alive. My identity has changed forever. I'm not of Scott and Jennifer anymore. I'm just Jennifer." She felt invisible in a world of couples.

Jennifer reluctantly faced the need to grow independent and make her own decisions. She redecorated several rooms and sailed on a cruise with friends. She relied on the verse that says, "I can do all this through him who gives me strength," which empowered her.

Another piece that helped her was reading books about others' grief—vicarious reading. To heal and cope, Jennifer poured out her emotions in a journal. A glimmer of hope finally appeared, ending days of despair when she realized she would make it after all. Another verse gave her optimism: "And the God of all grace, who called you to his eternal glory in Christ, after you have suffered a little while, will himself restore you and make you strong, firm and steadfast" (1 Peter 5:10).

Then Jennifer remembered how the ministry leader at her church assisted with the funeral and offered support throughout the following year. The new hope gave her a desire to assist others. She wrote, "I want to give back because of the help given me." She trained as a Stephen Minister and now co-leads a grief group in her church called Rebuild.

Grief transformed Jennifer in several ways. She learned to lean on Christ to give her strength when she felt she couldn't manage. Through her grief, she discovered a deeper sense of gratitude and appreciation. Now, she is using the unwanted gift of grief to help others with funerals and a grief support group. The grief work we do changes us and we grow in unexpected ways.

"All endings are also just beginnings.
We just don't know it at the time."

—Mitch Albom

God of strength,

Be my strength. May my grief transform me into a better person, enabling me to help others. I appreciate you and thank you for the people you have brought into my life. Amen.

Reflect: Ponder changes within you that stemmed from your grief.

Respond: Be open to God working through your loss.

Read: Ephesians 3:14–21

Journal Prompt: Describe one area of growth you see in yourself since your loss.

A Constant Companion

"May the God of hope fill you with all joy and peace
as you trust in him, so that you may overflow with hope
by the power of the Holy Spirit."

—Romans 15:13

> ### THOUGHT FOR THE DAY
>
> The Holy Spirit is our comforter.

EXPERIENCING THE LOSS of someone dear or facing a significant change can feel like being suddenly cast into the open air, like a free fall from an airplane. Our sense of balance disappears, and the foundation of our world seems to vanish beneath us. Questions arise: *How will we move forward? Can we endure this?* The life we once knew seems changed, daily routines feel strange, and the future remains uncertain. The sensation of falling overwhelms us—we can't see our landing spot, nor are we sure of surviving the fall.

Grief can flood in suddenly and unpredictably, stirring up a whirlwind of emotions. Like a free fall, there's nothing to hold on to, no hint of security, leaving everything uncertain, disorienting, and frightening. The good news is that we aren't alone when jumping from the plane. We have a tandem jumper with us.

Years ago, the nation watched as media outlets covered former President George H. W. Bush's historic skydive to celebrate his ninetieth birthday. Strapped to a certified instructor in a tandem jump, he took the plunge despite the limited use of his legs. The instructor, at the former president's side, controlled the free fall, deployed the parachute, and executed the landing.

When thrown into the unknown territory of grief, the Holy Spirit is much like a tandem jumper. Jesus sent the Holy Spirit to be our advocate, comforter, helper, and companion. After the resurrection. Jesus said, "All this I have spoken while still with you. But the Advocate, the Holy Spirit, whom the Father will send in my name, will teach you all things and will remind you of everything I have said to you" (John 14:25–26).

Furthermore, we find a cohort in the Holy Spirit who never abandons us, being a constant companion through all the waves of grief on our journey. Regardless of our emotions, the Holy Spirit accompanies us . Besides the Holy Spirit being at our side, the Holy Spirit gives us hope. "May the God of hope fill you with all joy and peace as you trust in him, so that you may overflow with hope by the power of the Holy Spirit." The Holy Spirit mysteriously heals and transforms us.

Hold on to the truth that you have a helper, the Holy Spirit to guide and comfort you.

"The Holy Spirit is my friend: he is always with me."

—Barbara Rainey

Spirit of the living God,

I look to you to be my companion on this journey, to comfort, guide, and help me. Please heal, transform me and fill me with hope. In Jesus' name, amen.

Reflect: Remember times when you sensed you weren't alone.

Respond: Visualize the Holy Spirit at your side as a friend.

Read: John 14:15–26

Journal Prompt: Describe when you felt God far away and what changed that.

Day 52

God Supplies Our Needs

"And my God will meet all your needs according to the riches of his glory in Christ Jesus."

—Philippians 4:19

THOUGHT FOR THE DAY

God meets our needs regardless
of our weaknesses.

"I DON'T KNOW what I'll do if I can't take care of my Mimi," Paul said, his trembling voice filled with frustration. After his wife of fifty-three years suffered a severe stroke, she lost the ability to walk or stand, relying on a wheelchair. Mimi's new condition required nursing home care. They lived on a limited income and were unsure how long their retirement and insurance would last.

Determined, Paul renovated his house to accommodate Mimi's needs, and after eighteen months, he welcomed her home. Mimi needed constant supervision, and with support from family and friends, Paul managed her health. His daughter quit her job to help care for her mother. Paul, a former marine, lacked a natural nurturing nature, but when he became the caregiver, he tended to his wife's health with compassion and cared for every detail.

He often worried about having sufficient financial means to provide for her. To his amazement, God provided for their every necessity, both physically and spiritually, as well as emotionally and financially. Paul could genuinely say, "And my God will meet all your needs according to the riches of his glory in Christ Jesus."

After four years at home, the unthinkable happened. Mimi experienced another debilitating stroke. She needed a feeding tube and returned to a facility. Paul wondered how he would manage, and yet once more, God supplied all their needs.

Besides the financial concerns, they both grappled with grief over Mimi's loss of independence and quality of life. Fear frequently overwhelmed Mimi, but she found strength in Isaiah 41:10: "So do not fear, for I am with you; do not be dismayed, for I am your God. I will strengthen you and help you; I will uphold you with my righteous right hand." This verse gave her comfort, mainly because her stroke affected the left side, and God held her right hand.

After eight years, Mimi took her final breath, leaving Paul to face a profound loss. Though comforted by the certainty that she had entered a better place as a believer, his sorrow ran deep. This time, he mourned for himself, learning to move through life without her. Once again, God met his need, healing his heart. He grieved for himself, and he learned to navigate life without her. God also supplied his emotional needs. In his weakest moments, he clung to the truth of 2 Corinthians 12:10: "For when I am weak, then I am strong."

God will supply your needs during this time of loss.

"Death leaves a heartache no one can heal.
Love leaves a memory no one can steal."

—Irish headstone

God, my provider,

We thank you for supplying all our needs and giving us strength when we are weak. Amen.

Reflect: Think of a time when God supplied your need.

Respond: Find a Scripture that gives you strength.

Read: 2 Corinthians 12:1–10

Journal Prompt: Write a letter to God telling him what you need emotionally.

Part 9

First Signs of Spring

Day 53

Jesus Provides Our Needs

"Ask, and it will be given to you; seek, and you will find; knock and the door will be opened to you."

—Matthew 7:7

PATTY ENDURED TWO devastating losses within a few years. Her first husband died after a prolonged illness. Later, she rekindled a childhood friendship that blossomed into love. They traveled, laughed, and envisioned a future as husband and wife. His sudden heart attack blindsided her, leaving her heartbroken and her dreams shattered.

After losing her childhood friend who had become her soulmate, Patty felt lost and unsure of where to turn. All her friends were couples, and her five sisters were married. For two months, she battled overwhelming loneliness. Finally, in desperation, she cried out in prayer, *Lord, I am so alone. No one understands me. Please bring just one widow into my life.*

The following week, a new woman walked into Patty's dance class who had lost her husband suddenly a few months before. God provided a widow friend for Patty.

Six days later, she attended the grief group I led, only to meet another widow who had also unexpectedly lost her husband. Patty attended a grief retreat at her church and recognized a man from her church who had recently lost his spouse. Patty joined a neighborhood women's Bible study, encountering several other widows. God had provided more than expected with several new friends who could relate to her.

Patty's story brings to mind the account of Jesus fulfilling the needs of his disciples after his resurrection. In John 21, the disciples set out to fish on the Sea of Galilee but toiled without a single catch. At dawn, the Savior appeared on the shore, though they failed to recognize him at first. He instructed them to cast their net on the other side of the boat. When they did, their net overflowed with so many catches they struggled to haul it in. When John and Peter realized it was Jesus, Peter immediately jumped into the water and swam to the beach to meet the Master. There, he discovered a fire with fish and bread already prepared. Christ welcomed them with the invitation, "Come and have breakfast" (John 21:12).

Just as Patty experienced God's grace, the Lord stands ready to provide for our physical needs and the deep longings of the heart: companionship, encouragement, and acceptance. He remains everpresent. Beyond earthly needs, Jesus offers to fulfill spiritual desires: hope, faith and peace. He reassures us, "Ask and it will be given to you; seek and you will find; knock and the door will be opened to you." Whenever loneliness comes, call out to Jesus. He waits with open arms.

"Tears shed for another person are not a sign of weakness. They are a sign of a pure heart."

—José N. Harris

Dearest Jesus,

You know my inner desires. Meet those longings, bring people to listen, and give hope when I can't see my way. Amen.

Reflect: Imagine Jesus on the beach, waiting for you.

Respond: Thank Jesus for answered prayer.

Read: Matthew 6:25–7:11

Journal Prompt: How has Jesus met your needs in the past month?

Day 54

Moving Toward Healing

"Surely he has borne our griefs and carried our sorrows; yet we esteemed him stricken, smitten by God, and afflicted."

—Isaiah 53:4 ESV

THOUGHT FOR THE DAY

Jesus walks with us in our pain
and brings healing.

BILL WALKED INTO the grief group and declared, "Once I get past this, I'll be fine." His wife had died just three months earlier, and he arrived expecting the group to offer a fix—something that would help him move on quickly and get back to life as he knew it. Gently, the co-leader and I responded, "Grief is a process, not something you simply move past."

For a long time, people believed grief followed a neat and orderly path—a sequence of stages leading to closure. Once a person reached "acceptance," it was assumed the journey was complete. But modern understanding tells a different story. Grief is not linear. It is cyclical, unpredictable, and deeply personal. We don't walk a straight path from pain to peace; instead, we often find ourselves revisiting the same emotions, sometimes within the span of a single day.

The emotional terrain of grief is more like a wilderness than a roadmap. One moment we might feel deep sorrow; the next, anger or guilt. Later that same day, we might experience moments of calm, only to be overtaken again by waves of anxiety or despair. The heartache of loss brings with it a wide range of emotions—sadness, rage, disappointment, hopelessness, fear, even moments of reconciliation—but they rarely unfold in an orderly fashion.

What makes this journey bearable is not just time to process, but presence—the presence of Christ, who meets us in our suffering. Scripture assures us, "Surely he has borne our griefs and carried our sorrows; yet we esteemed him stricken, smitten by God, and afflicted" (Isaiah 53:4). Jesus not only died for our sins; He carried the full weight of human sorrow. He knows the anguish of loss, the sting of separation, and the ache of the human heart.

Because of this, we can entrust our pain to him. We are not left alone to navigate the wilderness of grief. Christ walks with us in the dark places, offering grace, comfort, mercy, and peace. He does not promise to remove our suffering, but he redeems it—shaping us through it, gently transforming our brokenness.

Though the road may be long and winding, healing does come. By God's grace and with the slow, sacred work of grieving, we begin to emerge from the wilderness. Life will never be the same—but over time, we learn to carry our loss differently. The memory of our loved one remains, woven into our story. We find ourselves more empathetic, more compassionate, and often more willing to walk with others in their pain.

"God understands suffering because God has suffered."

—Jerry Sittser

Savior,

Thank you for carrying my pain and being with me in this grief. Give me peace and comfort in chaos. By your grace, bring reconciliation and healing. Please help me live in the present. Amen.

Reflect: Think about Jesus' suffering in the garden of Gethsemane and on the cross. He bore your source of grief.

Respond: Be aware that you will cycle through different emotions.

Read: Isaiah 53:1–12

Journal Prompt: Describe how your emotions cycle with your loss within a day.

Day 55

Jesus Is Always Present

*"Then their eyes were opened and they recognized him,
and he disappeared from their sight."*

—Luke 24:31

THOUGHT FOR THE DAY

God is carrying you in your grief.

"MY PHYSICAL HEALTH controls my life, and I don't like that," Christina admitted. Grief is often associated with loss, but when an illness transitions into a chronic condition, it can bring a different grief—one that affects daily life in profound ways.

Christina held the title of the youngest project manager in any company in the United States. She balanced a full-time school schedule and enjoyed fishing on the weekends, but debilitating migraines struck unexpectedly in her thirties, followed by a cascade of other health problems. Despite numerous medical appointments, surgeries, and medications, her symptoms never improved. Work became arduous, with 24/7 throbbing in her head and relentless body aches.

After getting laid off, Christina grieved as the life she once knew disappeared. She struggled with depression over losing her job and the realization that the life she had dreamed of was no longer possible. She felt crushed and defeated. As a result, she expressed, "Chronic pain leads to depression."

At the time, she couldn't see or feel God. Out of necessity, Christina moved in with her parents for support and to a city with better health care, including counseling. Her trusted dog, Trigger, remained a steady companion and comfort. She filled her days with creative outlets, designing flower arrangements for weddings and centerpieces as a way to bring her joy.

Her story evokes the account of two men journeying to the village of Emmaus after the crucifixion of Jesus. Sorrow overcame them because they placed their hopes in Jesus of Nazareth as their Messiah. After his death, those hopes seemed shattered. As they walked to Emmaus, a stranger joined them and shared the Scriptures concerning the Messiah. Upon reaching their destination, they invited the stranger to join them for a meal. As he broke bread with them, they identified the man as Jesus. "Then their eyes were opened and they recognized him, and he disappeared from their sight."

Christina didn't recognize Jesus when she lost her job and experienced multiple surgeries, but she realized later that he had carried her and planned her steps. "I'm exactly where God wants me. I just don't have to like it. His hand is leading me where I have to go." She wears a serene expression on her face now. Christina is reimagining her entire bucket list—embracing the blessings in her life and cherishing time with her parents. She recognizes she's not alone in facing difficulties, saying, "Everyone has challenges." Then Christina reflects with grace, "I've learned to accept the changes in my life." God enabled her to come to a place of peace and reconciliation with her loss.

Jesus is walking with you in your loss, whatever that might be.

"Perspective is everything when you are experiencing the challenges of life."

—Joni Eareckson Tada

Jesus,

Please help me to recognize you in my life, no matter the circumstances. Carry me daily, and bear my burden. Amen.

Reflect: Ponder the times when you have felt God carrying you.

Respond: Ask God to open your eyes to see Jesus.

Read: Luke 24:13–25

Journal Prompt: Describe a time when you knew Jesus was walking beside you.

Day 56

A Heavenly Perspective

"My flesh and my heart may fail, but God is the strength
of my heart and my portion forever."

—Psalm 73:26

THOUGHT FOR THE DAY

The Lord is all I need.

ERIC DISCOVERED THAT tears brought release and relief after he lost Betty, his wife of thirty-eight years, who died from breast cancer. They married young, raised two sons, and intertwined their lives together. After her death, he determined to move forward by selling their house and settling into a new neighborhood. He allowed himself time and space to grieve, often leaning on friends and church members the first year. He called his fogginess "grief brain" because he could only take one step at a time. Gradually, as emotional healing took place, he could deal with more. The laughter of his grandson became his greatest joy.

When he remarried several years later, he embraced the marriage as a gift from God—a new chapter filled with love and gratitude. However, he admits, "Grief still fractures me." Outwardly, life goes on, but beneath the surface, cracks remain. Although his life is complete, sadness strikes unexpectedly—like stepping onto a creaky stair, uncertain if it can bear his weight. The noisy step reminds him of his grief. When the weight of loss presses in, he lets the tears fall. He clings to his faith through it all and confidently knows, "My flesh and my heart may fail, but God is the strength of my heart and my portion forever." Despite the ache, Jesus is his treasure, and he trusts.

As a believer, Eric drew encouragement from Scripture, Bible studies, sermons, and the camaraderie of fellow believers. He rested in the confidence of Betty's faith and found peace knowing she stands before God. He said, "She is with Jesus. One image is that she is not hovering over us, watching her friends or me. Instead, I had the unshakeable perception that she was facing away from me and toward Jesus. She was whole and healed, and her earthbound story was past, completed."

In addition, Eric quotes the apostle Paul: "We are confident, I say, and would prefer to be away from the body and at home with the Lord" (2 Corinthians 5:8). Today, Eric prays and gives support to a group of widowers, often saying, "We who remain, without our wives, are the wounded ones in need of healing over the years. Our wives are safe and at peace, home at last."

"Tears are the silent language of grief."

—Voltaire

Sweet Jesus,

I understand that my pain will not last forever. When the ache comes, lead me to you, my strength and my security. In your name, amen.

Reflect: Review the progress you have made in your healing journey.

Respond: Rely and trust God to be your security.

Read: 2 Corinthians 5:1–10

Journal Prompt: Describe the last creaky step you experienced with your loss.

Grieving Before a Death or Loss

"Let the peace of Christ rule in your hearts, since as members of one body you were called to peace. And be thankful."

—Colossians 3:15

THOUGHT FOR THE DAY

We can express gratitude even in loss.

ROGER STARED AT Deborah, his face blank. She couldn't help but wonder what that expression meant. Then she began noticing small things that seemed difficult for him—like sorting his tools or packing a box. When he finally visited the doctor, the diagnosis was mild cognitive impairment. Later, it was confirmed as Lewy body dementia, a progressive neurodegenerative disease.

After her husband died, Deborah came to the grief group I led and with tears running down her face and a shaky, high-pitched voice, she shared her story. Her husband's decline was gradual over nine years, but within a few years, he lost his ability to take part in decision-making and simple tasks around the house. As a result, the responsibility of being the primary source of income, and of following through on the plans they had made to move, fell on Deborah.

In addition, Deborah grieved each step of his weakening and loss of competence. Along with the cognitive impairment came hallucinations, increasing confusion, and heightened agitation. She thought, "I wonder how many years we have left." Later, she realized there would be no more romantic dinners. It seemed Deborah felt constant sadness. This was anticipatory grief, grief before a loss.

When I asked Deborah how she managed her husband's illness, she said, "Thankfulness and gratitude got me through. I learned to think about what I have, not about what I don't have." She said she could look back and notice a thread of God's grace holding her up. Her son and daughter-in-law offered tremendous support. Deborah holds on to the words Roger spoke just before he went to the hospital: "I'm dying, I'm going to see Jesus." She feels grateful for Roger's peace and his trust in his Savior. The ICU physician suggested, "The most loving thing to do is to let him go home." Hospice staff, along with the hospice chaplain, walked with her during the final few days, for which she remains grateful and continues to be grateful for her marriage.

In low moments, she thinks of regrets, wishing she had handled things differently. She kept herself busy, like Martha, who was preoccupied with preparing the meal for Jesus, rather than sitting at his feet and listening, as Mary did (Luke 10:38–42). When she does stop to listen to the Savior, as Mary did, peace comes. Then she refocuses on being thankful for fifty-four years of marriage and says, "Let the peace of Christ rule in your hearts . . . And be thankful."

As Debra did, look at the things you have and be grateful.

"Some people are always grumbling because roses have thorns; I am thankful that thorns have roses."

—Alphonse Karr

Lord,

You're aware of how challenging my days are. Please help me to see the good I have. Help me be thankful in all circumstances and all relationships. Amen.

Reflect: Contemplate on God's past provision.

Respond: Offer a prayer of thanksgiving.

Read: Colossians 3:13–17

Journal Prompt: Make a list of people and circumstances for which you are thankful.

Part 10

Light Beyond the Cracks

Day 58

Always a Limp

"Therefore we do not lose heart. Though outwardly we are wasting away, yet inwardly we are being renewed day by day."

—2 Corinthians 4:16

THOUGHT FOR THE DAY

Grief leaves a mark but changes us.

JAY TENDERLY CARED for his beloved wife as she fought an arduous battle with cancer. The prolonged struggle drained him. Some tests revealed promising numbers, igniting hope, while on other days, her health plummeted without warning, shattering his spirit and leaving him utterly battered. Those were painful years.

I vividly remember visiting Jay and Cheryl, cherished friends of mine. Jay's weary face betrayed the deep anguish of watching his wife's gradual decline, yet he held his emotions close to his chest. His eyes, shadowed with exhaustion, revealed unspoken sorrow. The air in their home hung thick with love and an unbearable sense of impending loss.

After Cheryl's passing, Jay felt a sense of relief. The love of his life no longer suffered, and he no longer rode the emotional roller coaster. During the first year without her, thinking ahead seemed impossible, his mind in a dense fog. Navigating life alone was confusing, and his social world shifted, leaving him feeling like a ship adrift in a vast ocean.

Thirteen years later, Jay reflects, "There are still days or moments that bring unexpected tears." Even after profound healing, grief lingers like an ever-present shadow. He reflects, "I never quite break free from grief." Some moments stir emotions of sadness, but once he surrenders to the tears, a release follows. He describes himself as walking with a limp—forever marked by the loss of his beloved Cheryl.

A striking parallel unfolds in the book of Genesis, where Jacob grieves his deception of Esau, dreading and fearing of their impending reunion. Alone on the eve of their meeting, Jacob wrestles fiercely with an angel. The angel touches his hip, and from that moment on, Jacob walks with a limp—a lasting reminder of his struggle and transformation.

Like Jacob, losing a loved one irrevocably changes us, leaving us to traverse life with a limp. Wounded on this side of heaven, we move forward with a cane, always carrying the residual of loss.

Jay says, "I'm wounded this side of heaven and still walk with a cane." Yet even with a limp, Jay stands resilient, drawing strength and hope from the Holy Spirit. "Though outwardly we are wasting away, yet inwardly we are being renewed day by day." He testifies that grief reshaped him, deepening his compassion and self-awareness. Jay witnessed firsthand how the Holy Spirit faithfully renewed him daily. His loss didn't define him; it made him a stronger, faith-filled person.

As with Jay, God redeems our pain and loss, changing us for the better.

"The journey through grief is life-changing."

—Alan D. Wolfelt

Dear living God,

There is so much I don't understand. Please help me trust you and allow my grief to transform me into a stronger person. Amen.

Reflect: When have tears brought you an unexpected release?

Respond: Notice how you have grown from your loss.

Read: Genesis 32:22–32

Journal Prompt: How could grief continue to transform you?

Day 59

It's Been a Year

*"Remember the days of old; consider the generations long past.
Ask your father and he will tell you, your elders,
and they will explain to you."*

—Deuteronomy 32:7

> **THOUGHT FOR THE DAY**
>
> Recalling memories brings healing.

AS THE FIRST anniversary of my mother's death approached, I found myself overcome with dread. I couldn't help but wonder, *Will I panic? Will I be paralyzed by grief?* Her birthday and the holidays had already been emotional and January 11, the day marking one year, loomed ahead like a shadow.

I had been through a difficult loss before. My father died six years earlier, and the first year without him was filled with sadness and challenging. Still, losing Mom shook me in a different way, maybe because she was my last parent. I felt unmoored, as if I was drifting. My sense of identity, security, and belonging were shaken. I had to rediscover who I was without her. But in the midst of grief, I held tightly to the legacy she left me.

In the days leading up to January 11, I reached out to my two sisters. We talked and shared memories of Mom, remembering how special she was to us. I also decided to make a plan for the day itself, something meaningful that would help me honor her.

That day, I sat with my family and looked through old photo albums. We reminisced and talked of good memories. I created a shadow box with a piece of her jewelry. Now, each time I walk past it, I picture her wearing it and it brings me comfort. One of my sisters placed a photo of Mom on her desk with a single red rose, a simple but profound act of remembrance. These small gestures grounded us, helping us through the day.

That first anniversary reminded me just how disorienting loss can be. However, I learned that healing often begins with intentional remembrance.

The first anniversaries following any loss often bring anxiety and apprehension. All the "firsts"—the first Christmas, the first Easter, your birthday, and their birthday can be tricky to navigate. One of the best ways to face the dreaded days involves planning something to do or acknowledging your loss in some way. Devoting a few moments to remember, talk, or pay tribute to honor your loss can be therapeutic and promote reconciliation and respect. Tangible acts of remembrance help us process our grief and create space for peace.

Scripture offers us this encouragement: "Remember the days of old; consider the generations long past. Ask your father and he will tell you, your elders, and they will explain to you."

Now I have a tradition of looking at photo albums on the anniversary of my mom's death and calling my sisters. If you are approaching an anniversary, consider making a plan. It can be small but meaningful way to mark the day. It won't erase the grief but will remind you of happy memories and help you through the day.

"We bereaved are not alone. We belong to the largest company in all the world—the company of those who have known suffering."

—Helen Keller

Dear loving God,

When I fear another occasion will come around, surround me with your presence's embrace. Comfort me in your kindness and mercy. Amen.

Reflect: Remember a joyful time with your loved one.

Respond: Tell others what you need on that special day or an upcoming anniversary.

Read: Psalm 107:1–9

Journal Prompt: Write about a memory of your loved one or your loss.

Day 60

Hope Will Emerge in Darkness

"He will wipe every tear from their eyes.
There will be no more death or mourning or crying or pain,
for the old order of things has passed away."

—Revelation 21:4

THOUGHT FOR THE DAY

Recalling God's promises brings hope.

EVERY YEAR, WHEN I notice the first sprout of a bluebonnet, I say out loud, "How does this happen?" Something miraculous happens in March in South Texas after a cold winter, when the landscape is brown, trees are bare, grass is dormant. Everything looks bleak and cloudy. Before spring officially arrives, delicate blossoms burst from the hardened earth, signaling the promise of spring. First, a single bloom emerges in rocky soil. A few days later, fields transform into vibrant carpets of blue, purple, and periwinkle, thriving even in the most unlikely places along highways and in rugged terrain. Bluebonnets even appear in cracks in the sidewalk, the plants are determined to emerge. Then, I see other signs of spring, buds on the branches and the chatter of birds.

When we experience a loss, our hearts are heavy with sadness, loneliness, denial, self-doubt, anger, and shock. Grief resembles the dark winter of the soul. When circumstances seem grim or emotions ebb and flow, God comes, bringing a holy expectation called hope. Sorrow will lessen, and hope will arise, much like bluebonnet blossoms before spring. Hope will bloom in your heart. Within a week, one flower multiplies into an entire field of flowers.

We have the promise: "He will wipe every tear from their eyes. There will be no more death or mourning or crying or pain, for the old order of things has passed away." Someday, all sadness, including weeping and emotional and physical pain, will be gone because God will make everything new. The Holy One will dwell with his people, taking away death.

We can cling to God's promises by recalling and rehearsing them. "Let us hold unswervingly to the hope we profess, for he who promised is faithful" (Hebrews 10:23). God's assurances remain trustworthy, and he never fails.

When the first bluebonnet blooms, it signals the nearness of spring. In the same way, hope begins to stir—a sacred assurance that sorrow won't linger forever. Sometimes, it arrives gently, no louder than a whisper. Hold on to the whisper, recall God's promises and then your faith will grow.

"Hope is being able to see that there is light despite all of the darkness."

—Desmond Tutu

God of hope,

Please bring a holy expectation to my heart in this season of grief. You promised never to leave me and to comfort me. Help me grasp tightly to your word. Amen.

Reflect: Visualize the signs of spring and the changes it brings.

Respond: Anticipate hope to come like a bluebonnet sprout.

Read: Revelation 21:1–7

Journal Prompt: Write out several promises from Scripture that God gives us.

If you are unsure whether you are a child of God, refer to the appendix ("How to Have a Relationship with Jesus") for guidance on becoming one.

A Final Word

ALTHOUGH GRIEF IS universal, your grief is unique. You started your grief journey by entering an unknown wilderness with no trails. Initially, all seemed hopeless. However, as you walked, you came across a trail and saw light filtering through the trees. Finally, you left the wilderness, still carrying grief but now grief doesn't consume you. You possess new tools, personal growth and hope. The loss you experienced changed you, and you learned that grief is a journey with no finish line.

Elisabeth Kubler-Ross explains, "You will grieve forever. You will not 'get over' the loss of a loved one; you will learn to live with it. You will heal, and you will rebuild yourself around the loss you have suffered."

Be patient and gentle with yourself, reassuring yourself that you are making progress. I commend you for having courage to face your grief. You are a hero. Allow the Holy Spirit to comfort you along your journey. Revisit some of the devotions, as you will find new insights each time. Sadness will soften, and precious memories will emerge more often. We may not be able to have our loved one with us or to regain our loss but we have memories to hold. As someone once said, "When someone you love becomes a memory, the memory becomes a treasure." The final word is this: "He will wipe every tear from their eyes. There will be no more death or mourning or crying or pain, for the old order of things has passed away" (Revelation 21:4).

Appendix

How to Have a Relationship with Jesus

THIS SECTION WILL teach you how to connect with Jesus if you want a personal relationship with him.

We begin with the fact that we all tend toward sin, and no matter how much we try, we often fail, saying something hurtful, doing something wrong, or thinking impure or hateful thoughts. We can't be good enough to be right with God. We need help!

We then recognize that all of us have sinned against God, and because of that, we fall short of God's standard of righteousness. "There is no difference between Jew and Gentile, for all have sinned and fall short of the glory of God" (Romans 3:22–23). Our sin separates us from God.

"For the wages of sin is death, but the gift of God is eternal life in Christ Jesus our Lord" (Romans 6:23). But God provided a rescue through Christ.

Although we have sinned, Christ died for our sins and provided a way of escape. "But God demonstrates his own love for us in this: While we were still sinners, Christ died for us" (Romans 5:8).

When we acknowledge Jesus as our Lord and that he died for our sins, God hears us. At this point, receive Jesus' gift of him dying for us. It is not ours until you receive it. The best way to receive the gift is to pray.

"If you declare with your mouth, 'Jesus is Lord,' and believe in your heart that God raised him from the dead, you will be saved. For it is with your heart that you believe and are justified, and it is with your mouth that you profess your faith and are saved. . . . 'Everyone who calls on the name of the Lord will be saved'" (Romans 10:9–13).

Here is a simple prayer:

Dear God,

I realize I have sinned against you, and no matter what I do, I can't be good enough. Forgive me for my sins. I repent and need your help. I believe Jesus came, died for my sins, and was raised from the dead. I ask Jesus to be my Lord, Savior, and friend. Come into my life, Jesus; I want a relationship with you. Please help me follow you and obey you. Be real in my life. Thank you. In Jesus' name I pray, amen.

Now, with God's help, you can live to honor God, draw closer to him, and be more loving to others. Share with a fellow believer what you just prayed so they can help you in your next steps in following him.

Topical Index

THE FOLLOWING INDEX refers to the Day number instead of the page number.

Despair/Discouragement

Divorce

Doubt/Questions

Faith/Trust

Fear

Forgiveness

Gratitude

Guilt/Regret

Holidays

Hope

Loss of a Dream

Loss of a Friend

Loss of a Grandparent

Loss of Health (Physical or Mental) or Disability

Loss of a Parent

Loss of Self or Self-Doubt

Regret/Guilt

Rest/Peace

Security/Love

Stages of Grief

Sudden Death

Suicide

Surrender

Recommended Reading List

Grief in General

Alan D. Wolfelt, *Understanding Your Grief: Ten Essential Touchstones for Finding Hope and Healing Your Heart* (Companion Press, 2021).

Ann Voskamp, *The Broken Way: A Daring Path into Abundant Life* (Thomas Nelson, 2016).

Barbara Brown Taylor, *Learning to Walk in the Dark* (Harper One, 2015).

C. S. Lewis, *A Grief Observed* (Seabury Press, 1961).

C. S. Lewis, *The Problem of Pain* (Simon & Schuster, 1996).

Jerry Sittser, *A Grace Disguised: How the Soul Grows Through Loss* (Zondervan, 2021).

Joni Eareckson Tada, *A Place of Healing* (David C. Cook, 2015).

Judy Pelikan, *The Heart's Journey* (Abbeville Press, 1996).

Kenneth C. Haugk, *Journey Through Grief from Stephen Ministries* (Stephen Ministries, 2023).

Kenneth J. Doka and Amy S. Tucci, *Transforming Loss*, (Eds) (Hospice Foundation of America, 2018).

Laura Story, *I Give Up: The Secret Joy of a Surrendered Life* (W. Publishing Group, 2019).

Mark Vroegop, *Dark Clouds, Deep Mercy: Discovering the Grace of Lament* (Crossway, 2019).

Prayers and Promises for Grief and Loss (BroadStreet Publishing, 2020).

Timothy Keller, *Walking with God through Pain and Suffering* (Penguin Books, 2016).

Tony Evans, Chrystal Evans-Hurst, Priscilla Shirer, Anthony Evans, and Jonathan Evans, *Divine Disruption: Holding on to Faith When Life Breaks Your Heart* (Thomas Nelson, 2021).

Children in Grief or Crisis

Joseph M. Primo, *What Do We Tell the Children? Talking to Kids about Death and Dying* (Abingdon Press, 2013).

Karen Dockrey, *When A Hug Won't Fix the Hurt: Walking with Your Child Through Crisis* (New Hope Publishing, 2000).

Laura Dower, *I Will Remember You: A Guidebook Through Grief for Teens* (Scholastic Inc., 2001).

Chronic Illness, Loss of Health

Laura Story, *I Give Up: The Secret Joy of a Surrendered Life* (W. Publishing Group, 2019).

Lori Ann Wood, *Divine Detour: The Path You'd Never Choose Can Lead to the Faith You've Always Wanted* (Lori Ann Wood, 2023).

Comfort

Kay Arthur, *When the Hurt Runs Deep: Healing and Hope for Life's Desperate Moments* (WaterBrook, 2012).

Max Lucado, *Safe in the Shepherd's Arms: Hope and Encouragement from Psalm 23* (Thomas Nelson, 2009).

Max Lucado, *You'll Get Through This: Hope and Healing for Your Turbulent Times* (Nelson, 2015).

Daily Devotions

Dawn Daily, *From Grief to Grace: A 40-Day Devotional on Healing from Loss* (Dawn Daily, 2020).

Debbra Sell Bronstad, *52-Week Devotional Journal for Grief: Prompts and Prayers for Navigating Loss* (Rockridge Press, 2022).

Erin Cushman, *Bright Hope: 28 Daily Devotions for Grief in Light of the Gospel* (Bright Hope, 2020).

L. B. Cowman (ed.), *Streams in the Desert: 366 Daily Devotional Readings* (Zondervan, 1997).

Leslie J. Thompson, *In This Season: 30 Daily Devotions to Renew Your Faith in a Time of Grief* (Living Bridge Press, 2022).

Mattie Jackson, *Through The Valley of Grief: A 365-Day Devotional of Spiritual Practices for Hope in Suffering* (WaterBrook, 2024).

Max Lucado, *You Can Count on God; 365 Devotions* (Thomas Nelson, 2021).

Morgan Cheek, *Even in Darkness* (Paper Peony Press, 2021).

Nancy Guthrie, *The One Year Book of Hope* (Tyndale Momentum, 2005).

Sara Perry, *365 Days of Prayer: for Grief and Loss* (BroadStreet Publishing, 2021).

Twila Belk, *Raindrops From Heaven* (BroadStreet, 2015).

Daily Practical Suggestions

Alan D. Wolfelt, *365 Days of Understanding Your Grief: Daily Readings for Finding Hope and Healing Your Heart* (Companion, 2021).

Martha W. Hickman, *Healing After Loss* (Harper Collins Publishing, 1994).

Shelby Forsythia, *Your Grief, Your Way: A Year of Practical Guidance and Comfort After Loss* (Zeitgeist, 2020).

Death of a Child

Bekah Bowman, *Can't Steal My Joy: The Journey to a Different Kind of Brave* (Can't Steal My Joy, 2019).
Jerry Sittser, *A Grace Disguised: How the Soul Grows Through Loss* (Zondervan, 2021).
Nancy Guthrie, *Holding on to Hope: A Pathway Through Suffering to the Heart of God* (Tyndale House Publishers, 2002).

Death of a Spouse

Jerry Sittser, *Grace Disguised: How the Soul Grows Through Loss* (Zondervan, 2021).
Mattie Jackson, *Through the Valley of Grief: A 365-Day Devotional of Spiritual Practices for Hope in Suffering* (WaterBrook 2024).
Rachel Faulker Brown and Never Alone Widows Team, *His Name: Our Hope in Grief: A 30-Day Devotional* (Be Still Ministries, 2022).

Infertility

Ali Forrest, *Anchored in Hope: Devotions for Infertility* (2015).
Deb Hall, *Barren and Beautiful: Discovering Joy and Healing in the Wake of Infertility* (2021).
Nancy Canestrari Williams, *A Crocus in the Desert: Devotions, Prayers and Stories for Women Experiencing Infertility* (Lightbourne Creative, 2019).

Pastoral Care and Professional Resources

Darcy Harris (ed), *Non-Death Loss and Grief: Context and Clinical Implications* (Routledge, 2020).
Alan D. Wolfelt, *Death and Grief: A Guide for Clergy* (Accelerated Development Inc.,1988).
Granger E. Westberg, *Good Grief* (Fortress Press, 2011).
Ingrid Kohn and Perry-Lynn Moffitt, *A Silent Sorrow: Pregnancy Loss* (Routledge, 2000).
Jane Heustis, and Marcia Jenkins, *Companioning at a Time of Perinatal Loss* (Companion Press, 2005).
Kenneth C. Haugk, *Don't Sing Songs to a Heavy Heart* (Stephen Ministries, 2018).

Kenneth J. Doka and Amy S. Tucci (eds*) Transforming Loss; Finding Potential For Growth* (Hospice Foundation of America, 2018).

Kenneth J. Doka and Amy S. Tucci (eds). *Beyond Kubler-Ross: New Perspectives on Death, Dying, and Grief. Hospice Foundation of America*, 2011.

Kenneth R. Mitchell and Herbert Anderson, *All Our Losses, All Our Griefs* (Westminster John Knox Press, 1983).

Leslie C. Allen, *A Liturgy of Grief: A Pastoral Commentary on Lamentations* (Baker Academic, 2011).

Tim P. VanDuivendyk, *The Unwanted Gift of Grief: A Ministry Approach* (Haworth Pastoral Press, 2006).

Pregnancy Loss

Abby Wedgeworth, *Held: 31 Biblical Reflections on God's Comfort and Care in the Sorrow of Miscarriage* (The Good Book Company, 2020).

Adriel Booker, *Grace Like Scarlett: Grieving with Hope After Miscarriage and Loss* (Baker Books, 2018).

Erin Cushman, *Bright Hope: 28 Daily Devotions for Grief in Light of the Gospel* (Bright Hope, 2020).

Sarah Philpott, *Loved Baby: 31 Devotions Helping You Grieve and Cherish Your Child After Pregnancy Loss* (Broad Street Publishing, 2017).

Acknowledgments

I BEGAN WRITING this book as a way to process my experiences during patient visits while serving as a chaplain. After each day, I would come home and write down their stories, searching for and discovering the quiet gems of faith and hope within them. I called those gems "Unexpected Glimpses" of God at work in their lives.

I am honored by the people who allowed me to share their loss stories. Their names have been changed to protect their privacy. Their stories are compelling and carry genuine sorrow and grace.

I am humbled by my chaplain mentors at the Metropolitan Methodist Hospital, where I worked, Rev. Edmund Knott, Rev. Lance Burk, Sister Bernadette Bezner, and Father Michael Fitzgibbon, who all contributed to my growth as a chaplain.

I am indebted to the writing groups who listened to my stories. First, the Hill Country Retreat Writing Group allowed me to explore my writing abilities. They listened and, above all, were my cheerleaders, giving me the confidence I needed—a special thanks to Ed Douglas, who started the group. Second, I am indebted to my writing critique group, Word Weavers, precisely page 40. The gals in the group encouraged me and critiqued my work. Thank you, Carrie, Norma, Lynda, Allison, and Loretta.

I am blessed to have my prayer partners who prayed for me during the writing of this book: Bekah, Susan, Sharon, Ed, Linda, Judy, and Cindy.

I am thankful for three additional women whom I will never forget: Rev. Sue White, Fay Green, and Rena Seligman—Sue, an encouraging mentor who gave me courage to step out in ministry; Fay, a professional grief counselor, who taught me so much about grief and the grieving process; and Rena, a counselor who helped me believe in myself when my sons with disabilities were young.

A special thank-you to the team at Illumify Media Global for their valuable help in publishing this book, especially Michael

Klassen, who held my hand through this process and read every devotion.

I am profoundly grateful and blessed to have my family. My parents, Frank and Aleta, who encouraged me to write and believed in me. I am grateful for my sons, Joel and Chris, who allowed me to share part of their stories. My dear husband, Walter, gave me space to write and assisted with technology. He offered thoughtful feedback and unwavering support. Without his faith in my passion for capturing these stories, this book would not exist.

About the Author

CHARLEEN BURGHARDT IS a teacher and a board-certified chaplain. She taught for years and then later worked for over a decade in hospice and hospitals as a chaplain, walking with many in loss and death.

She planned on teaching her entire career. However, life changed when she had two children with special needs and a rare disease. As a result, she became a strong advocate for people with disabilities. Her passion for helping others led her to pursue a master's degree in Christian education from Southwestern Baptist Theological Seminary and a residency in clinical pastoral education. Charleen leads grief groups, teaches workshops, and speaks on various topics. In addition, Charleen writes for periodicals and support groups. She is an elder in her denomination.

San Antonio, Texas, is home for Charleen and her husband, Walter. They have three adult children. She is available for speaking.

Connect with Charleen

Check out her Website/blog: https://CharleenBurghardt.com

Email her at: char.burghardt@gmail.com